What people are s

Questioning Sp

In *Questioning Spirituality: Is It Irrational to Believe in God?* Eldon Taylor offers a remarkably thoughtful and wise reflection on the tensions between matters of faith and of science. While our society has become increasingly secular and less religiously engaged or affiliated, questions of faith, spirituality, meaning, and the beyond have not gone away and are frequently on the minds of many. During increasingly turbulent and rather apocalyptic times due to climate change, economic inequality, a global pandemic, divisive politics, war, and other deeply disturbing challenges, questions about spirituality and faith become even more salient, even among those who are identified as "nones" or "dones" when it comes to organized religion. Dr. Taylor's many years of experience, scholarship, reflection, and wisdom are evident throughout this book and anyone who is engaged by questions of meaning, purpose, and the beyond would likely find plenty to chew on within these pages.
**Thomas G. Plante, PhD, ABPP,** Augustin Cardinal Bea, S.J. University Professor

In this book, Eldon Taylor provides a compelling read for anyone struggling to reconcile matters of faith and spirituality with logic and scientific rationality. His discussion blends elements of neuroscience, psychology, philosophy, and religion in addressing the question as to whether or not it's irrational to be spiritual or to believe in a Higher Power. Offering a non-dogmatic approach, he objectively examines both the inconsistencies and benefits of religious practice and belief. When it comes specifically to considering the role that spirituality should or should not play in life, anyone craving food for thought will find nourishment here. Though Taylor argues that it is pragmatically rational and advantageous to believe in a Higher Power, any final decisions are left up to the reader.

**Anthony Falikowski, PhD,** author of *Higher Reality Therapy*

In *Questioning Spirituality*, Eldon Taylor takes the reader on an intellectual safari investigating two competing worldviews, and he provides explorations and explanations of each perspective that are fair, honest, and insightful. In some respects, there is competition between naturalism and spirituality, while in others there is a confluence that some readers may find surprising. We certainly learn through empirical observation of the natural world, but that does not preclude the possibility that paragnosis and noetics may also provide avenues to understanding the place that humanity occupies within our world. Perhaps the world of matter and energy is not the world entire. Other phenomena may also matter. From ancient philosophers to contemporary scientists, Eldon Taylor surveys some of the brightest lights illuminating the questions and debates at issue. He concludes that belief or unbelief is still very much what William James called a "genuine option." It is not irrational to believe that there is something more than can be identified with telescopes and microscopes. Spirituality is not for the scientifically benighted or for mere wishful thinkers. Investigate the matter for yourself, and you may find that contemporary dismissive attitudes toward faith and spirituality are simply not warranted by the available evidence. Taylor encourages his reader to investigate the matter carefully, modestly, and honestly. This is always wise advice, and Taylor's *Questioning Spirituality* is a crucial contribution to our explorations of the human condition. Highly recommended!

**William Ferraiolo, PhD,** Philosophy Department, San Joaquin Delta College

*Questioning Spirituality* is an inspiring read. While Eldon is unafraid to expose the problems in absolute "belief," whether it is the belief in science or in religion, he does it in a way that brings hope and peace to all. *Questioning Spirituality* is not about finding some compromise that leaves both theists and atheists feeling dissatisfied. Instead, it is a synthesis of beliefs that brings forth something that is truly freeing. It seems believing in science does not have to mean abandoning faith and believing in spirituality does not require blind faith. Examine, question, and then choose for yourself.

**Marci Shimoff,** #1 *New York Times* best-selling author of *Happy for No Reason*

Eldon Taylor explores interesting and thorny issues, such as free will, and the sometimes-conflicting accounts of religious events. He threads his needle and pushes it into one buttonhole after another, striving for simplicity, rationality, and even comfort in whatever one might personally define as a "spiritual" belief. I enjoyed his "white crows" analogy because while many of us have never seen evidence of a god or a spirit world, we've never seen radio waves either. A book that provides food for thought and exploration for atheists like me, and theists all.

**Ingrid Newkirk,** President of *People for the Ethical Treatment of Animals*

I have known Dr. Eldon Taylor as a colleague for over 35 years. His research and recordings have proven to be helpful to many individuals and are a major contribution to the self-help field. Dr. Taylor's new book *Questioning Spirituality* is especially relevant today as many of us wrestle with issues of faith in light of the invasion of Ukraine and a 21st century holocaust.

His insights can provide the reader clarification and perspective in evaluating how they live their own life. By asking us to examine our own belief systems, Dr. Taylor offers us tools to navigate and perhaps reevaluate how we live our own life. Highly recommended.

**Steven Halpern, PhD,** Grammy® nominated recording artist, sound healer, and author

For too long now, my love of science has meant that I had to deny those feelings inside that kept telling me there is more to life than science can demonstrate. My need to be considered smart and rational meant I had to ignore those experiences that defied sensible explanations — experiences that we have all had at some time or another. With clear simple logic, *Questioning Spirituality* demonstrates that believing in a spiritual life is no more irrational than not believing in it. This knowledge means that the exploration of spirituality is no longer taboo for those of us who consider ourselves to be hard scientists or intellectuals — being open to spirituality is no longer a betrayal of our scientific standards. With the playing fields now fully leveled, I realized I finally had permission to fully embrace the spiritual side of my life. This shift in thinking is incredibly freeing!

**Seema Chaudary,** Lab Technician

"Scientism" was pushed on me when I started college in the 1970s. It was equated with being a good person, or so I believed. But since then, I have noticed that Science believers have the same weaknesses and biases as other humans. This brain we've inherited is hard to manage. It's tempted by immediate rewards even though it can conceptualize more lasting rewards. Dr. Taylor's book is a valuable tool for confronting this challenge.

**Loretta Breuning, PhD,** author of *Habits of a Happy Brain*; founder Inner Mammal Institute

*Questioning Spirituality: Is It Irrational to Believe in God?* provides a thoughtful summary and reflection on some of the most essential topics within the field of psychology, including the power of hope, the role of genes, and the connection between mind-body. Readers interested in learning more about the science of happiness, and in particular the insights from neuroscience on how our thoughts and practices can literally change the brain, will find this book particularly engaging and inspiring.

**Catherine Sanderson,** POLER Family Professor and Chair of Psychology at Amherst College

# Questioning Spirituality

Is It Irrational to Believe in God?

# Questioning Spirituality

## Is It Irrational to Believe in God?

Eldon Taylor, PhD

Winchester, UK
Washington, USA

JOHN HUNT PUBLISHING

First published by O-Books, 2023
O-Books is an imprint of John Hunt Publishing Ltd., 3 East St., Alresford,
Hampshire SO24 9EE, UK
office@jhpbooks.com
www.johnhuntpublishing.com
www.o-books.com

For distributor details and how to order please visit the 'Ordering' section on our website.

A CIP catalogue record for this book is available from the British Library.

Design: Lapiz Digital Services

UK: Printed and bound by CPI Group (UK) Ltd, Croydon, CR0 4YY
Printed in North America by CPI GPS partners

The author of this book does not dispense medical advice or
prescribe the use of any technique as a form of treatment for
physical, emotional, or medical problems without the advice of a
physician, either directly or indirectly. The intent of the author
is only to offer information of a general nature to help you in
your quest for emotional and spiritual well-being. In the event
you use any of the information in this book for yourself, which is
your constitutional right, the author and the publisher assume no
responsibility for your actions.

We operate a distinctive and ethical publishing philosophy in
all areas of our business, from our global network of authors to
production and worldwide distribution.

# Contents

## Dedication

To my sons, Roy and William
And to all of those who have found themselves lost,
lacking hope, but still asking the big question.

# Preface

A popular argument in educated circles today essentially insists that a belief in a higher power is but superstitious mumbo-jumbo nonsense. Indeed, when you follow through on the writings and public debates, the argument's critical bottom line can be put this way: It is fundamentally irrational to believe in a god of any kind.

Irrational is defined as "unreasonable, illogical, groundless, baseless, unfounded, unjustifiable, unsound." It is the purpose of this work to show that not only is a belief in a higher power sound, but it is also a healthy alternative to that offered by atheists. Indeed, in many ways it is more rational to believe than not.

We live at a time when more and more people find themselves identifying with a form of scientism. To them, the religions of old offer candy-man appeal with little basis in logic or science. Further, these people have often been inculcated, especially in higher learning institutions, with the idea that secular progressive thinking represents the only reasonable worldview. To many then, it is simply irrational to believe in a higher power. This has led a growing number to become disappointed in life, and the data bears this out, particularly with Gen X and Millennials, who in increasing numbers are seeking meaning by becoming nuns or entering the priesthood.[1] That said, altogether too many of these people are left lost, depressed, and missing meaning.

There are many problems inherent to some of the old ways of defining God, religion, and spiritual practices. Scientific peers such as Christopher Hitchens, Michael Shermer, Richard Dawkins, Sam Harris, Daniel Dennett, and so forth are quick to take the cheap easy shots. The fact is, a belief in a higher power, in an afterlife, is not dependent upon outmoded thinking and/

or archaic definitions. That said, understanding where many of those affected by the prominent atheists/agnostics of our time find themselves necessitates opening this work where they are. It is for that reason that Chapter One begins by assessing some of the ideas of the past, especially those most criticized and fairly so. It is my hope that, by meeting those who have given up on the reasonableness inherent in a belief in an afterlife, or a higher power—by meeting them right where they are, I can pave a path into a deeper understanding of what might be, and more specifically, the benefits that are gained from a belief in a higher power.

As you will see, it is my position that if we are outcome-oriented with our choices in life, then how we choose to live our lives, what we choose to believe and why, should inherently bear benefit. If we truly wish to be intellectually honest, then we would recognize in the get-go that we cannot prove the unprovable, and as such, to take up the position of an atheist is incoherent with intellectual honesty—for to say there is no god and be unable to prove the same is just as unsound as to say there is a god and fail to be able to prove it. Thus, we are therefore forced to the position of offering good reasons to be either agnostic or believer. Additionally, as alluded to earlier, I hope to also demonstrate through the use of logic that belief in a higher power is not irrational at all; indeed, it is the more rational of choices.

Now, I will tell you up front that *Questioning Spirituality* was written for two primary audiences. The first is for the young adult who has been educated away from religion because of all of its inconsistencies, and in some instances, nonsense teachings, but who nevertheless would like to find a deeper meaning to their lives. The second is for the parent/guardian who is unable to argue with the logic their educated children present to them— logic that basically states that if religion cannot stand toe-to-toe with science, then it must be false.

I wrote this book first and foremost for my own two sons. I felt that in their pursuit of science they were discarding the aspects of life that I found the most important. The inner spiritual life brings a whole host of benefits ranging from health and wellness to peace and hope. Without spirituality, life becomes just a rat race that we can never win. It is my heartfelt desire that my sons experience the riches that can be found in spirituality. To reach my boys though I had to understand where they were coming from, to fully acknowledge the problems inherent to most formalized religions. If I ignored these issues, then I knew my sons would not be able to see the validity of my arguments for spirituality.

It is for these reasons that *Questioning Spirituality* is divided into three parts: thesis, antithesis, and synthesis. Part One puts forward the thesis, facing head on the obvious problems with religions. As such, this may be particularly difficult for people of faith, as it will appear that I am knocking their most fundamental tenets. I would ask that you bear with me. In Part Two, I present the other side of the issue—the antithesis. Education tends to hold science as almost sacrosanct for it holds all the logical answers—but does it? In my examination of science's view on spirituality, I uncover the basic flaws that most do not bother to look at. With the negation of thesis and antithesis, new opportunities open up for a third way— synthesis—that place where the benefits of leading a spiritual life far outweigh the path of the coldness of science that doesn't offer any meaningful answers anyway.

Now, one more important point. I have been blessed by many who willingly gave of their time to review the material in this work. One reader suggested that the book perhaps portrayed "a father venting his frustrations over his sons' choices." Nothing could be farther from the truth. Both of my sons are no longer atheists. Indeed, our conversations and willingness to understand each other, and communicate honestly, is the very fabric that distilled the work you are about to read. In fact, my son William wrote a review of the book that explains more, and you will find it in Appendix A.

If you are a parent and wish to communicate with your children about religion and spirituality, you will find many ways to do so in this book. Whatever the reason you have this book in your hands now, may you know peace, balance, and joy!

Thank you,

*Eldon*

# Introduction

*What I fear most is power with impunity.*
*I fear abuse of power, and the power to abuse.*
~ Isabel Allende

More and more people today have turned their backs on religious institutions. While religion has been declining, secularism has been surging. There are many reasons for this, but I am convinced that three major ones exist—first, most religions fail to deal adequately with scientific findings; second, the tautological and inconsistent logic incorporated in the so-called mysteries (mandates/definitions) are held out as axiomatic *truths*; third, the neutrality with respect to religion attempted in public schools. It is my intention to both clarify the problems, flesh them out fully so there's little doubt that they're understood, and then unpack the *hows* and *whys* behind certain manmade relics of organized institutions that can seem more intent on power and control than on spirituality. To that end, I will begin with the indoctrination process and continue through the primary secular complaints inherent in religious skepticism.

When someone asks me what religion I follow, and I inform him or her that I am an interdenominational minister, they typically have a follow-up question, "What does that mean?" The answer is simple: I do not profess to offer *a* path. Instead, I believe you can find value, beauty, and truth in most religions and spiritual paths. That said, organized religions tend to create problems for themselves by way of their doctrines and covenants. Further, some organized religions seek to convince their followers that they have the *only* right way. This exclusivism separates, divides, and betrays the inclusive view that we are all in this life together. Historically, religious differences have resulted in some of the world's most horrific acts, to say nothing of the lives that religious wars have taken.

I like to explain that it is the spirit of spirituality, the essence of brotherly love and respect for all life that is at the core of my learnings. This sometimes leads to questions that reveal how little some folks understand about spirituality. In the minds of some, to be spiritual and not belong to some organized religion translates into new age meandering. By that I mean, take a little of this, some of that, add that which feels good, and call that spirituality in the name of personal truth. I have no real issue with this, for shopping around is one way to inform yourself, to learn, and to grow. That said, grabbing something simply because you wish it were true, or it feels good, or your all-wise guru says it's so, is a certain way to find yourself lost in the variety of confusion that exists in much of the new age use of ancient occult teachings and the modern social movement.

I have enjoyed the love of two wonderful sons. I have also watched them change from agnostic to atheistic as they finished their college education. Both of my sons were raised with a belief in a higher power, albeit more the idea of the intelligence that permeates our universe than an anthropomorphic being. They were not indoctrinated with the traditional dogma found in so many religions, but rather taught a respect for all life and an expectation of a life in the hereafter. Both of my sons were present when many unexplained events took place in our home. Indeed, I wrote a book *What Does That Mean?*, detailing the many special events in my life that defy science-based explanations, events I refer to as white crows, in the hopes that they would devour the material and that this alone would persuade them to believe in something more than the materialistic reductionist view foisted on people in most universities today. Alas—I failed.

As such, it occurred to me that, in order to reach my sons, I needed to enter the woods where they are and understand *why* they believe as they do. Is it possible to find commonalities in our life philosophies? By examining the two opposing beliefs, will it be possible to find the deeper truths: thesis, antithesis, synthesis? To that end, I have dedicated this work to my sons, Roy and William.

# Part One: Thesis

## The Antagonist Arguments: Why Not to Believe

*Whoever is careless with the truth in small matters*
*cannot be trusted with important matters.*
~ Albert Einstein

It is unreasonable, indeed irrational, to believe in God or some sort of higher power. Science has explained the human condition, its evolution, and how consciousness arises. There is no reasonable basis to retain the idea of a God, a so-called Grand Organizing Designer. The fact is, science has more than adequately explained why people are so susceptible to accepting religious dogma. As Freud once put it, "Religion is a sugar-coated neurotic crutch," one many choose to cling to rather than discard to stand on their own.

# Chapter 1

# Indoctrination

*Education is not merely neglected in many of our schools today,*
*but is replaced to a great extent by ideological indoctrination.*
~ Thomas Sowell

I was raised Mormon. I read the texts, repeated them for many Sunday talks, entered the priesthood, blessed the sacrament, became a junior assistant scoutmaster under our church ward's sponsorship, and so forth. In other words, I was a model Mormon youth. Despite attempting to mirror the desired model, I had many questions.

In time I entered seminary school, which in those days was supported by the public education system in Utah. As such, my seventh-period class in high school was seminary. I knew that here I would finally obtain the answers to the many issues that troubled me. I asked many questions and very often was instructed in a stern manner, "Refrain from the mysteries."

I scored well on my homework and tests and deserved an A, but when the grades were handed out, I discovered I had received an F. I took this grade to the school principal. The next day I met with my seminary teacher, the president of the seminary, and the principal. In that meeting, they told me that I could have the grade I earned if I never went back to seminary.

I can't express how disillusioned and disappointed I was with this outcome—I took the grade and never returned. In my mind, I had just been effectively excommunicated for asking questions that were deemed a "disruptive influence on the class."

## Disruptive Questions

If God is all-knowing (omniscient), does this mean, as some Protestants assert, that God already knows what we will do and has therefore already decided who will be saved and who will not be? Is that a fair question—or a disruptive one? If God is all-powerful (omnipotent), why wasn't Adam created with a perfect will? Or did God intentionally create Adam with a deficient will so that Adam would be sure to sin? If so, what does that say about free will? Is this an inane question that should not be asked? Or how about, if God is all-good (omnibenevolent), why are there tidal waves, birth defects, earthquakes, and other so-called natural calamitous affairs that claim so many every year? Why do bad things happen to good people? Are these really unfair questions to ask? Are they truly so disturbing that church leaders would choose to separate the questioner from the flock in order to protect those who fail to think about what they are regurgitating?

## Accommodating Science

Ask a question about the differences between science and religion and you will either be told to ignore science, since it fails in some way or another, or some variation will be added to the teaching, such as with intelligent design. For example, the Bible informs us that in the beginning God created everything ex nihilo—from nothing. Evolution informs us of a different creation story.

To accommodate this, a religious teacher may choose to tell us that God works through natural law, so evolution is compatible with the creation story. According to this view, God created the earliest life and allowed it to evolve naturally. However reasonable this may sound at first blush, how does it account for Eve being taken from the rib of Adam? Ask this and you're right back into the mystery. Object on the basis you've been taught the Bible is the literal word of God, and you'll likely find yourself out in the cold alone.

## Dubious Neutrality

In an effort to separate church and state in our public school system and eventually even in those old, traditional, religiously established universities, our educational system has leaned toward secularism. In the words of Paul James Toscano, as stated in his law review article titled "A Dubious Neutrality: The Establishment of Secularism in the Public Schools", various Supreme Court rulings have led educational institutions to "maintain an intellectual environment entirely devoid of religious ideas and influence."[2]

## Inconsistencies

The problem with religious systems is that they refuse to look at the inconsistencies in their teachings, and people today are just too bright to buy into the old pat answer, "Refrain from the mysteries."

Still, life itself is a mystery. Who am I? Why am I here? Is it all just a matter explained by the materialistic reductionist theories found in science? Are we but meat machines who evolved to reach what most think of as the pinnacle of the evolutionary ladder? Is our reasoning ability only an emergent property of the brain, or is there a mind that is capable of operating in ways that at least appear to be non-local?

In short, are we spiritual beings, or are the secular preachers correct and the belief in life after death or God is just, as Freud put it, "A sugar-coated neurotic crutch."

This book is about my own journey and reflections on what I have learned, come to believe, and why. I sincerely hope it aids the readers in some small way with their own struggle for meaning in what can often seem like a somewhat meaningless life.

# Chapter 2

# What to Believe

*It's very difficult to distinguish between what a person believes and what they say they believe.*
~ Daniel Kahneman

Testimonial evidence among the members of the group can be a powerful persuader. Testimonials are another convincer in that they become part of the legendary nature of our otherworldly beliefs. Jesus raised the dead, cast out the demons, walked on water, and so forth. The miracles many choose to believe form the anchors on which their belief web is spun.

## Miracles

Miracle stories are common to all religious organizations, and today we find them emerging anew in new age movements. For example, the new age prophet Annalee Skarin ascended before her followers. Mark Prophet, the husband of Elizabeth Clare Prophet, founder of Summit Lighthouse, ascended. J.Z. Knight, founder of Ramtha's School of Enlightenment, channels an ancient Lemurian warrior who fought the Atlanteans some 35,000 years ago.

Are these miracles and are they to be taken literally? Are they any different than the miraculous stories we find throughout all of religious history? After all, religions tell us some pretty stupendous and similar-sounding stories. Here are just a couple of examples. The Bible informs us that Enoch ascended in a chariot of fire, and Moses was immediately transfigured.

Christians celebrate the birth of Jesus on December 25 to the Virgin Mary. A star in the East guided three kings to his birthplace. He was a prodigal teacher and started his mission at age thirty. He had twelve apostles and performed many miracles, such as walking on water, healing the sick, and turning water into wine. He was crucified and then resurrected three days after he died.

However, Horus, too, was born on December 25, to a virgin mother (Isis) and a star in the East (Sirius) pointed the way for three kings. He was a prodigal teacher at age twelve and began his mission at age thirty. He was betrayed for thirty pieces of silver, crucified, and was resurrected three days after he died.

In 1200 BCE, Mithra of Persia was born to a virgin on December 25. He had twelve disciples, performed miracles, was dead for three days, and then resurrected.

In 500 BCE, Dionysus of Greece was born to a virgin, was referred to as God's only begotten son, performed miracles such as turning water into wine, died, and was resurrected.

In fact, a short list of such stories would include Zoroaster, Indra, Balai, Beddru, Krishna, Buddha, Odin, and more.

## Belief

How true do you think these stories are? Are they anchors in your own belief system, or have you discarded them long ago and become somewhat of a skeptic when it comes to miracle stories? If so, are you just a jaded person who now looks on spiritual matters with the eye of a cynic?

In my view, it is difficult today to believe in a higher power since both common sense (in light of the history of religion and the nature of our human psychological needs) and the sciences have a much more Occam's razor-style interpretation, and logic itself forces conclusions that deny traditional arguments and/or definitions.

So where does that leave us? Are we to deny our rational minds and ignore the authority in science if we are to be spiritual? Or are we to integrate the explanations offered by science in some new version of our spiritual belief? For instance, as mentioned earlier, it's not uncommon today for religiously thinking people to combine evolution with creationism — offering an explanation that allows for God to work through natural laws, and that includes evolution. This order of thinking has God creating the beginning of all things but allowing nature to evolve the human being to a state where God then infused homo sapiens with a soul.

How much evolution do you think the various religions of the past have had to undergo in order to survive? We've all heard the tales of Galileo attempting to share his telescope with the senior cardinals only to have them refuse to look. Are we to imitate the cardinals and refuse to challenge those beliefs we hold most sacred? If not, then is it possible to reconcile a spiritual belief in today's world? Ultimately, one must ask, is it irrational to be a spiritual person? We'll examine that question in the chapters to follow.

The truly spiritual path begins by learning about ourselves. After all, if we human beings are created in God's image, then to ignore an understanding of ourselves is to overlook the obvious.

# Chapter 3

# The Meaning of Truth

*Absence of evidence is not evidence of absence.*
~ Carl Sagan

What is truth? Is there only one truth about a subject or are there many? How often have you heard someone say something like, "I have my personal truth"? What is a personal truth? Is it valid to have personal truths? I'm forced to say that subjective interpretations of objective events entitle us to something— an opinion, a belief, but not necessarily a "truth." Truth can be evasive. There are, of course, so-called hard truths such as 2+2=4, albeit math is a discovered language, and we don't speak it perfectly for there are some kinds of math where we *assert* that 2+2=4, but we can't *mathematically* prove it. That qualification added, many truths are relative in the sense that there is no observable or provable way that can be agreed upon for truthful assertions of this nature. Even at that, one might counter that no two things are identical, so how can two of anything other than the abstraction, the number two, equal two of anything else?

## Choosing Your Truth

Everyone today seems to have his or her own "truth." What does that mean? These personal truths are invariably subjective in nature. How is a personal truth verifiable? What does the word "truth" mean when it's a subjective personal matter?

Organized religion and personal spiritual beliefs both have their alleged truths. As discussed in the Introduction, these truths are often self-contradictory. However, even worse is the so-called personal truth, for it knows no reason per se. By that I mean, there is no logical way to disagree so one either rejects or accepts based on their own personal bias. If it sounds good, and/or feels good, then we are inclined to want to believe and even share the truths of others.

The manifestation of a miracle is an example of truths many wish to believe. There could be many possible explanations that call upon natural laws to explain the miracle, but we tend to ignore these if we are predisposed to hope for miraculous interventions in life. That said, when there is no acceptable explanation, we either discard the matter as anomalous unessential artifacts or incorporate the material into life-changing events. Indeed, my own research has led me to conclude that where many people experience anomalous events, they often repress them. Perhaps this is because they fear ridicule, but more on this later.

## Credibility

So, we live in a world where most of the scientific community has accepted that we are but meat machines who have evolved through millions of years of trial-and-error vis-á-vis Darwinian selection processes, and everything about us and our world is explainable via the natural sciences. According to science, religion is superstition fraught with nonsense and fed by ignorance—one may as well govern their day-to-day life by that which is printed in the local paper's horoscope section.

Religiously minded people, by contrast, ignore this rhetoric, often at their own peril. It's easy for one to become so lodged in a belief as to be unable to release it even when the belief is proven false. Social psychologists conduct experiments demonstrating this phenomenon on a regular basis. For example, research has repeatedly demonstrated that when a news story reveals some bit of information that we approve of, say, a negative item on a politician we dislike, that even when they run a retraction, we continue to believe the original story.[3]

The mind is a complicated matter. Our beliefs are a web of interconnected strands attached to anchors that we have inherited from our enculturation, our social engineering, our self-feedback assurance, our defense mechanisms, our compliance needs, as well as our participation with, and acceptance or rejection by, our fellow tribe members.

There is safety in numbers, goes the old saying. Collective beliefs provide numbers that reinforce our beliefs. When the expert speaks, such as your physician, you give this more authority and therefore more credibility than what you hear from a workmate. When ten doctors tell you the same thing, it's fact! But is it?

## Truths Can Lie

Hector Macdonald shared many ideas with me regarding truth. His book, *Truth: How the Many Sides to Every Story Shape Our Reality*, informs us of how truth should have an ethical hierarchy. In other words, there are many truths, and we can find ourselves cherry picking the truths that serve our agenda or biases. As Hector told me, "Truth can be used to lie."

One of the stories Hector tells in his book has to do with Colgate toothpaste. Colgate sent questionnaires to dentists asking them to identify the toothpastes they recommended. When the questionnaires were returned Colgate announced that 80% of dentists recommended Colgate. This, in turn, persuaded other dentists to begin to recommend Colgate as well. Why? Because research once again shows that people follow the herd, and nowhere is this better illustrated than with the line length study. In this study, subjects are asked to identify the larger of two lines. However, four or five confederates, those who are in on the experiment, choose a shorter line as the longest. The experimental subject, who begins by properly choosing the true longest line, soon begins to follow along and deny their own senses in so doing. As the confederates choose the shorter line, so does the experimental subject.[4]

Now here's the thing with the Colgate advertising campaign. There were many types of toothpaste recommended by the dentists. In other words, the dentists did not *only* recommend Colgate, they may well have also listed several other brands in their survey, but Colgate did not include that information. Eighty percent may well have also recommended Crest, for example, but Colgate did not report the other brands recommended. As such, they told the truth, but the truth did not represent all of the facts.

Cherry picking facts is what we all do when we defend a position. When our herd, our tribe, collectively holds to the same interpretation, it can be exceedingly difficult to let go of the belief, the "truth," that we hold dear to our being. But cherry picking is not the only problem we face when trying to learn the truth.

## Knowing

Imagine that we have six witnesses from whom we are collecting evidence. One witness states emphatically that the accused broke into her home. The next witness is equally adamant that the accused was home in bed with her at the time in question. Another witness states that they saw the man crawl through a ground-level window as they were passing in their automobile, and yet still another witness questions the certainty of that statement by pointing out how poorly lit the area is. However, they, too, had seen something from their home across the street, but by the time they dressed and got outside, the accused was kneeling on their neighbor's front lawn. Still another witness insists that this is the man they caught in their home and held until law enforcement arrived. And our last witness claims that the accused was home in bed all the time.

Now, when law enforcement arrived, the accused was kneeling in the front yard with a gun pointed at his head by the owner of the home allegedly entered illegally by the accused.

The accused argues that he saw someone running from the house and the homeowner ran outside in pursuit and mistakenly identified him as the burglar, threatening to shoot him if he didn't kneel and remain stationary until the cops arrived.

## Perception of Truth

We are all aware of the problem that can arise from eyewitness testimony and the variety of descriptions that witnesses can provide. Our system of justice simply could not work if the descriptions offered by every witness were all taken to be absolutely true. The fact is what we are dealing with is the perception of truth by each of the witnesses.

I have reported in the past on people who truly believe what they offer is the truth despite the fact that the evidence says something else altogether. I have also shared stories of our propensity to believe what we want to believe. Often weaved in both scenarios is the construct known as cognitive dissonance or the notion that we can hold two mutually exclusive ideas simultaneously and never recognize this dissonance. For example, I have an acquaintance who accepts natural selection but holds fast to the Bible as the literal word of God. These two beliefs are mutually exclusive as we have already noted.

I'm sure you have no problem noting that the witnesses' testimonies in our little example cannot all be true. So, it is with truth—or we need to change our meaning of the word. Thus, when you next hear something like, "That is my personal truth," recognize that, as with the witnesses, they are describing the truth according to their perception—and that is all they are describing.

## Not Truths

Perception is an interesting human faculty in that science has clearly shown that many shared illusions, preferences, beliefs, and so forth literally reinforce false perceptions. Indeed, in some instances of mass hysteria, groups of people have been known to fall ill with the same symptoms, such as a rash, high temperature, or abnormal blood counts. In one such instance of mass psychogenic illness, several people reported symptoms that included dizziness, muscle cramps, tremors, and shortness of breath. This occurred in Beirut at a time when the city was under near-constant threat of violence, and the case was reported to the Saint George Hospital University Medical Center, where the attending health-care professionals finally diagnosed the problem as "mass psychogenic illness (epidemic sociogenic attacks)."[5]

Perception is not truth—and sometimes it is a lie. It can be false to fact. If we are to become awake, it is incumbent upon us to seek the truth. Truth seekers recognize the many possible paths others call truth, but they are unwilling to accept the herd definition and rather continue their journey seeking that ineffable and perhaps undiscoverable epistemological certainty.

Bottom line, getting to the truth of any matter is not quite as simple as one might think. The nature of experience further complicates this, since for all of us, what we experience is *truth* in the sense that we *know* we just experienced it. Of course, we could have dreamed it, imagined it, and so forth—so given the ambiguous nature of truth when it comes to the metaphysical side of spirituality, hard truths are hard to come by. We can question historical information, attack cosmic rhetoric with logic, etc., but the nature of truth in any meaningful metaphysical enquiry is one best left to the art of philosophy.

Chapter 4

# Who Am I?

*There's something safe about playing a character, but then it's like,*
*"Who am I underneath it all?"*
~ Emmy Rossum

One of the oldest questions ever asked is simply, "Who am I?" Moses asked God, "Who are you?" and God answered, "I am that I am." Since there is no such thing as a statement that fails to contain a question, or a question that fails to contain a statement, what happens if we turn God's answer around? Seen as more than an answer, the question becomes, "Who are you?" Can we answer that question the same way, "I am that I am!"

The question, "Who am I?" can be said to be so trite that no one takes it seriously. Oh, we all have our pat answers, such as, "I'm Eldon Taylor, male, writer, inventor, businessperson, etc." We can fill in all the blanks, when and where we were born, our parents' names, perhaps even our genealogy, where we live, a physical description, etc. This, however, does not approach the real meaning of the question, "Who am I?"

## Why Am I Here?

Many disciplines have tried to answer this question. Perhaps we are unable to answer the question, but if so, I think this might be the case because we tend to think of ourselves in lofty ways whenever we entertain deeper meanings. One could say, we are products of evolution driven to preserve our DNA, ever procreating for that purpose. In order to produce as many copies as possible we compete with others driven to do the same thing, and this leads to fear, anger, and eventually violence. When we die, all that remains is the DNA in our offspring and perhaps a short-lived memory of who we were. For many, *this* is the answer to our question—is it yours?

Others think in terms of eternal life and that can become truly complicated. For some, it means the possibility of purgatory; for most, it means a state of blissful happiness. What this blissful happiness *is* depends greatly on your definition of happiness. Some believe happiness is eternal progression, ever learning and becoming wiser and perhaps even gods. Some hold the old classical view of angels and harps, but as Mark Twain once said, paraphrased, "Who wants to go somewhere where all there is to do is sit around and listen to harps playing?"

## Eternal Life

In any event, whatever the lofty eternal view of one's quintessential self, soul, spirit, etc. may be, the answer to the question "Who am I?" usually takes on the form of glittering generalities in that it fails to answer the individual question and reverts to generalizations about eternal life. Perhaps that's fair—perhaps we're all essentially the same and there is no room for individual personalities. Is that what you think?

What if the entire question, the search for *who I am*, is a fool's folly? What if the notion of "I" is but an illusion? What if our sense of self, our idea of an eternal self (soul) is but our way of dealing with the inevitable, and yet lifelong avoidance of death? What if we are nothing more than an emergent property of a material accumulation of the physical world, organized in such a way as to give rise to the illusion of mind?

Let's now go down the rabbit hole—a deeply serious rabbit hole, one that leads to the very center of the most meaningful question ever asked by man: Who am I?

## Inability

Douglas Hofstadter in his book, *I Am a Strange Loop*, suggests that human beings have two things going for them with respect to their sense of *I-ness*. One is an ability and the other an inability. The ability is self-reflection—a sort of special servo-loop that remembers the past, exists in the present, and thinks about the future. This special ability generates the notion of *I-ness* for we begin to see ourselves as the actors who participated in the past and plan the future in the present. (This is an extremely simplified version of Hofstadter's *ability*, but since it is not the thrust of our discussion, I'll just encourage you to read his book.)

Our discussion here is directed at emergent properties; in particular, those that we refer to as consciousness and soul. Therefore, I want to focus on Hofstadter's *inability*. What is this inability? In a few words, we are unable to even think adequately about the level of our being, where everything begins and where every day is run by the system that we think of as ourselves. Our consciousness (sense of self—being) is a loop, checking itself by using the loop, so we are trapped in this circularity.

For centuries the world could not imagine that something we could not see could kill us. The idea of bacteria was absolutely foreign, let alone the notion of cells, DNA, RNA, and the like. Indeed, in the fifth century the Greek philosopher Leucippus of Miletus and his student Democritus of Abdera postulated the idea of a substance that could not be divided, and they named it the *atom*. Centuries later we thought we had confirmed the smallest unit and gave it the name *atom*. However, it wasn't long before the atom gave way to still smaller units participating in the generation of our physical world.

## Consciousness

Think about your consciousness—no, think about your brain. What level of action in your brain gives rise to consciousness? Is it the neurons, the synapses, the neurochemicals, the atomic substrate underlying the electrochemical interactions, or what? Of all these physical actions—which are conscious? Do you control them?

Let's think about a fine instrument, or better still, a very sophisticated robot. This robot—we'll call her Charlie—has an advanced Artificial Intelligence (AI), so advanced that for all intents and purposes, it almost seems human. You come home and it greets you with a glass of wine, a cup of tea, your favorite single malt whiskey, or whatever your preferred beverage is. It takes your coat and hat, briefcase, lunchbox, and/or whatever is appropriate and puts it away for you. It sits down and converses with you, "How was your day?"

Now think about Charlie for a moment. Charlie is not conscious as you believe yourself or other human beings to be. Charlie's body, despite its soft skin-like properties, is a built-up mechanism. Charlie's intelligence is artificial—existing on a framework of zeros and ones. All that undergirds Charlie's appearance as a moving, thinking thing is simply a matter of a deeper and unseen organization of non-conscious matter.

Now let's think again about being human. All that undergirds the operation of our I-ness is built from non-conscious stuff. That is, the atomic level, the electromagnetic aspect, even to a larger scale, the action of neurons, is non-conscious by nature. However, as a result of its accumulated action, an awareness arises. The awareness begins to loop back on *itself* and thereby considers itself. This *itself* emerges from non-conscious action by non-conscious units of energy and matter, and yet, when it considers itself, it assumes something—that something we call self-awareness or consciousness. In other words, we have the emergence of consciousness, or what we think of as consciousness, all as a matter of the action of non-conscious units.

## Emergent Property

Now with this understanding we find that mind is but an emergent property. The notion of soul also becomes an emergent property. Indeed, everything we think of as existing independently of the materialistic perspective inherent to all life is but an emergent property of an emergent property: *I-ness* or consciousness.

The ramifications to the proposition that we are but an emergent property can be mind-boggling. I mean, think of the many moral issues that are impinged upon via this realization. If humanness is but an emergent property, then what could be wrong with cloning humans, unlimited stem cell research, abortion at any stage of pregnancy, and so forth? The fact is, if our consciousness is only an emergent property, then the world we know from entertainment to education changes drastically. Is that bad?

It seems to me that consciousness as an emergent property also extinguishes what most think of as free will. Our consciousness would be a matter of programming, perhaps some nature, some nurture, some as nothing more or less than the memories of our ancestors.

What does the evidence say? Do we have free will?

# Chapter 5

# Free Will

*Life is like a game of cards. The hand you are dealt is determinism;*
*the way you play it is free will.*
~ Jawaharlal Nehru

Many scientists inform us today that the mind is an emergent property of the brain, that near-death experiences (NDEs) are simply a product of a dying brain, that we are but animals who are the product of millions of years of evolution, and that the notion we are anything more is but a neurotic crutch. Religion is nothing more than wishful thinking—paraphrasing the philosopher John Wisdom for a moment, "Doesn't it make you feel good? Isn't it like having Daddy at the end of the hall ready to turn your light on and protect you from the Boogeyman?" Or in the words of the noted agnostic Michael Shermer, "Religious faith depends on a host of social, psychological, and emotional factors that have little or nothing to do with probabilities, evidence, and logic."[6]

Many insist that the idea of God is simply incoherent in numerous ways. It's not just the definitional stuff, as discussed earlier; it's also the matter of a timeless being creating everything ex nihilo (from nothing). As Sean Carroll argues in his book *The Big Picture*, the Big Bang theory does not state that the universe came from nothing. Comparisons of God's creation to the Big Bang are patently absurd! Carroll, a physicist, points out that all the Big Bang theory states is that there was a time when time equaled zero. Does that mean that there were things and no time? The fact is, if you have two objects, then you have distance, and if you have distance, you have time. (How long does it take to get from object one to object two?) Additionally, even if you have just one thing, it still takes time to get from one side to the other, so *no time* would require there to be *no thing*, and the universe would therefore come from nothing. So, are we to take all of these objections seriously, and if not, what are we to do?

What to believe? The world is full of ugly matters. People seem quite capable of killing one another for very little reason. History is full of the cruelest deeds imaginable, including genocide, perpetrated by the one "made in His image" and other devout believers. This is often explained as a matter of free will, or the so-called "Best Worlds Argument." The argument informs us that man was created with free will, and God therefore allows us to exercise our autonomy accordingly. However, as will be discussed later, free will is questionable. Many prominent scholars today do not believe that free will exists. Indeed, when I asked Frans de Waal (the Charles Howard Candler Professor of Primate Behavior at Emory University) directly about free will, his answer was plain and simple and accompanied by a chuckle, "Free will is an illusion!"

## Choice

We have all been educated to believe that we choose our destinies. A criminal is someone who made different life choices from those who have never been convicted of a serious crime. Do I do A, or do I do B? Choosing is what our lives are supposed to be all about, but are they, and if so, in what way and to what degree?

I have enjoyed several robust conversations on my *Provocative Enlightenment* radio show with many of today's brightest thinkers, and there seems to be little difference in how they see the question of free will. Indeed, this might be a fair representation of their differences. For Professor Dick Swaab, author of *We Are Our Brains: A Neurobiography of the Brain from the Womb to Alzheimer's*, "Free will is only an illusion." For Julien

Musolino, author of *The Soul Fallacy*, it's all about "flexible will," meaning it is all a matter of the foundation program in our subconscious and our ability to change it, but largely speaking, it's still an illusion.

## Illusion of Choice

Why do the experts suggest free will is an illusion? Don't we all make choices, know that we're choosing, and act accordingly? Don't we all labor under the assumption that if we made different choices, our life might be different? Don't we all think that we can make new choices tomorrow and change our lives? After all, isn't a large part of our lives committed to being better people, better parents, improved businesspeople, and so forth? I suspect that most everyone who might ever read this book has made resolutions—resolutions to lose weight, stop smoking, learn a new language, read more, or in some other way improve their lives. Are these not conscious choices that we make? If so, what is meant by the illusion of choice—the illusion of free will? What's more, if you're going to try to sell free will as an illusion, are you saying everything is predetermined in some way?

Science comes to the conclusion that free will is truly nonexistent on the basis of experimentation. The fact is, studies have shown that an fMRI technician watching the brain in live time while you make a decision will know what you are going to decide seconds before you consciously make that decision. Indeed, there is a very disconcerting video produced by the BBC where Professor Marcus du Sautoy (Oxford University) demonstrates this fact. (A simple search for Neuroscience and Free Will, BBC will bring up several places you can view the video for yourself.) Now you might ask, as I did, how is that possible?

## Mind Programming

It is the content of our subconscious that makes most of our decisions, and the fact is, we are unaware of that content. In part, that content is the result of all the input our subconscious has received. In a very real sense, it is as computer programmers put it, GIGO—garbage in, garbage out. Think of all the programming, the advertisements, the political rhetoric, the religious insistence, the cultural imperatives, the rejections, rebukes, embarrassments, and so forth that form your beliefs.

Our minds, the subconscious repository of all we have learned, experienced, loved, and feared, together with our defense strategies, mechanisms, and basic drive-related needs— all of this in one mix, one broth, one cauldron consciously unknown to us—and it is actually making our choices.

A little history may be of use here. The neuroscientist Benjamin Libet carried out a series of experiments in the 1980s where he regularly observed that activity in the part of the brain known to be unconscious *preceded* the voluntary movement of muscles. This research appeared to inform us that unconscious processes precede conscious will.[7] This sparked great debate and triggered the entire notion that called free will into question.[8] Now many have since criticized Libet's experiments, arguing they were flawed.

Libet's work employed multi-cranial EEG technology to observe cortical evoked potential, or action potential. The debate continues somewhat today, but the use of fMRI appears to confirm the findings of Libet nearly a third of a century later.[9] As such, much less debate about the matter exists today for the undeniable fact is that at least 90% of our decisions are made in the unconscious—and that number is probably grossly understated. Nevertheless, because of this small part of our decision-making process that is available to each of us, I prefer to think of the matter not as one of free will, but rather one of *conscious* will. That said, there continue to be those who strongly reject the conclusion that free will is illusionary. "For example, Mele (2009) and O'Connor (2009) argue that the data adduced by researchers in this area wholly fail to support their revisionary conclusions."[10]

## Twin Research

So, let's look a little deeper and see what we can learn about this idea of predestined or predetermined. What may predispose us and to what extent? Are our genes involved? Does epigenetics play a role, and if so, how? I mean, could the memories of our parents, grandparents, etc. actually be transferred in our genes and influence our lives as well?

Identical twins are considered by many to be a living epigenetic experiment. Epigenetics is misunderstood by some, so let me take a moment to explain it. The NIH defines epigenetics this way:

DNA modifications that do not change the DNA sequence can affect gene activity. Chemical compounds that are added to single genes can regulate their activity; these modifications are known as epigenetic changes. The epigenome comprises all of the chemical compounds that have been added to the entirety of one's DNA (genome) as a way to regulate the activity (expression) of all the genes within the genome. The chemical compounds of the epigenome are not part of the DNA sequence, but are on or attached to DNA ("epi-" means above in Greek). Epigenetic modifications remain as cells divide and in some cases can be inherited through the generations. Environmental influences, such as a person's diet and exposure to pollutants, can also impact the epigenome.[11]

As such, evaluating similarities between identical twins separated at birth provides a true insight into the heritability of characteristics other than physical similarities. This situation may be more common than one might think. "Since 1922, there have been 1,894 cases of sets of twins reared apart, according to a study by [Nancy] Segal."[12]

What does this research show? Take this case reported by Segal:

In 1979, Jim Springer and Jim Lewis, "the Jim twins," were reunited at age thirty-nine after not knowing the other existed.

As described in Segal's book on the identical Jim twins, *Born Together—Reared Apart*, both had been adopted and raised by different families in Ohio, just 40 miles apart from each other. Despite their separate upbringings, it turned out that both twins got terrible migraines, bit their nails, smoked Salem cigarettes, drove light blue Chevrolets, did poorly in spelling and math, and had worked at McDonald's and as part-time deputy sheriffs. But the weirdest part was that one of the Jim twins had named his first son James Alan. The other had named his first son James Allan. Both had named their pet dogs "Toy." Both had also married women named Linda—then they got divorced, and both married women named Betty... The Jim twins inspired the *Minnesota Twins Reared Apart* study, which Segal also worked on from 1982 to 1992. This research once again showed surprising similarities in identical twins' habits, interests, intelligence, and religion despite their separate upbringings.[13]

## Sins of the Father (Epigenetics)

Think a moment about the notion often referred to as "sins of the father." The Bible informs us according to Exodus 20:5, "You shall not bow down to them or serve them, for I the Lord your God am a jealous God, visiting the iniquity of the fathers on the children to the third and the fourth generation of those who hate me." However, later in the Bible we can find many verses such as this one from Deuteronomy 24:16, "Fathers shall not be put to death because of their children, nor shall children be put to death because of their fathers. Each one shall be put to death for his own sin." So, what is the story here? Are we to think that only those who hate God are to be visited by the sins of their father?

Epigenetic research informs us that experience is passed down to our offspring. For example, "Where one's ancestors lived or how much they valued education, can clearly have effects that pass down through the generations. But what about the legacy of their health: whether they smoked, endured famine, or fought in a war?"[14]

"Biologists first observed this 'transgenerational epigenetic inheritance' in plants. Tomatoes, for example, pass along chemical markings that control an important ripening gene. But, over the past few years, evidence has been accumulating that the phenomenon occurs in rodents and humans as well. The subject remains controversial, in part because it harkens back to the discredited theories of Jean-Baptiste Lamarck, a nineteenth-century French biologist who proposed that organisms pass down acquired traits to future generations. To many modern biologists, that's 'scary-sounding,' says Oliver Rando, a molecular biologist at the University of Massachusetts Medical School in Worcester, whose work suggests that such inheritance does indeed happen in animals. If it is true, he says, 'Why hasn't this been obvious to all the brilliant researchers in the past hundred years of genetics?'"[15]

According to research carried out at RMIT University, "... dad's diet before they conceive could be genetically passed onto the next generation, with a subsequent impact on those children's mental health."[16] And that's the tip of the proverbial iceberg.

## Influence of Genes

Many scientists argue that criminality is largely inherited. Indeed, "After examining the DNA profiles of almost 1,000 criminals, two particular genes were found to be associated with violent, but not non-violent, behaviors."[17] Like many issues of this nature, scientists are quick to balk at the idea that it's in our genes— genetics made me do it. The subject is somewhat like the free will argument, for most scientists today believe that free will is non-existent. That said, the problem is that when science discusses matters such as genetics and free will in this context, it provides a defense for bad behavior, and no one really wants to go there.

Still, the ideas of original sin, something Lamarck argued as present in our genes, together with the behavior, environment, and even memories (or memes in the words of Richard Dawkins[18]) of the parent, are gaining momentum today. So, what if our genetic makeup predisposes us in certain ways—does that necessarily mean that our genes have absolute control?

Study after study of identical twins reared apart has revealed substantially the same genetic influence as that reported by Segal with Jim Lewis and Jim Springer. Despite this, twin research also shows a good deal of variance. The fact is, as geneticist Carl Bruder of the University of Alabama at Birmingham puts it, "I believe that the genome that you're born with is not the genome that you die with—at least not for all the cells in your body."[19]

Bottom line, we all have opportunities to improve our lot in life and we all can work toward doing just that, and for that reason, I am convinced that we are not destined to live out a life limited by our inheritance. I, for one, know firsthand that you can change your lot in life.

In a conversation with Mark Wolynn, an expert on this matter and the author of *It Didn't Start with You: How Inherited Family Trauma Shapes Who We Are and How to End the Cycle*, he suggested that once you recognize the inherited nature of genetic memory and its influence, you can identify these anxious feelings and desensitize them. In other words, you have the ability to save yourself and your children from suffering. Nevertheless, how considerable will the education necessary to do this be in order to avert the future potential for many epigenetic tragedies? Further, how much discipline and/or intervention technology will be appropriate? In other words, and by way of just one example, if you carry those so-called criminality genes and wish to live a non-criminal life, what must you know and do?

## Crime and Punishment

So, let's return to this idea of free will—an idea central to the proposition of justice. Punishment is based on the notion that we could choose differently. Is that really true and if so—is it equally true among all? Think, for example, of the difference between one born in a culturally rich environment versus one born into depravity in every sense. Their relative abilities would most certainly arise largely out of their educational/informational data set together with their DNA programming. In some subcultures, even in our western high-tech world, the idea that one might alter the expression of their DNA is considered nonsense. "God made you the way you are for a reason!" might be the argument.

Obviously, epigenetics, like many other advances in science, seriously challenges traditional religious beliefs. Does that mean, as some today argue, that religion is but a form of fossilized fortune-telling rubbish? Is it, as Freud remarked, "Religious doctrines... are all illusions. They do not admit of proof, and no one can be compelled to consider them as true or to believe in them."[20] After all, how do we reconcile the absence of free will with the prescribed crime and punishment system spelled out in the Bible, the Quran, the Torah, and so forth? Indeed, is it not a compelling argument to insist that man's sin is God's sin because he made us this way? I mean, if God is all-powerful (omnipotent) then he could have created us with a perfect will—at least theoretically. Furthermore, given the issues of free will and gene inheritance, does it not seem like we are hardwired to behave in ways that affirm God's intention— the world is predetermined, and we are but predestined pawns in the game? Is this how we should view the world?

How is a spiritually intelligent person supposed to respond? Atheistic pundits have gained great traction with some or all of these questions, as they rightly should. Therefore, for spirituality to be viable, it must not only admit the fatal characteristics inherent to some doctrines, but it also has a responsibility to define a reasonable means, purpose, and goal.

It's worth noting that there is an accumulating body of research that shows once a person accepts the idea that they have no free will, their behavior changes. Indeed, they become less honest and more aggressive. For example, quoting Alfred Mele, a Lucyle T. Werkmeister Professor of Philosophy at Florida State University,

The first study that was done on this was done by Kathleen Vohs and Jonathan Schooler, a pair of social psychologists. What they did was to divide their subject pool into three groups, and one group was given a passage to read saying that there's no free will, and another group was given pro free will passages, passages saying that you do have free will. The third group was given neutral passages, passages having nothing to do with free will. Then the next task was to take a math quiz and the subjects were told that the program was glitchy so that if they didn't press the space bar right after the questions showed up, then the answer would pop up on the screen, in which case of course, they could cheat because they could see the answer. What they discovered is that the group who read the no-free-will passages cheated way more often than the other two groups. The other two groups behaved about the same, which is evidence that free will is a kind of default assumption. They did a version of this study in which for correct answers you got a dollar for each one, and so by cheating you were stealing, and the people who read the no-free-will passages then stole more often than the others.

In another, Roy Baumeister, a psychologist at Florida State University, did a similar study. What he did was to divide the subject pool into two groups, and one group read passages saying that there's no free will, and the other group read neutral passages, and then the next task was to serve snacks to people who were about to walk into the room and the subjects were told two things about these people who are going to walk in. One, they've all indicated that they really hate spicy food, and two, they have to eat everything you put on their plate, and the group who read the no-free-will passages doled out way more of the spicy salsa option than the other group did. So, here again, lowering confidence apparently in free will increases misbehavior, and the misbehavior in this case is aggressive behavior causing people pain and suffering by giving them food they don't like that they have to eat.[21]

So, what is the relevancy of this whole discussion regarding consciousness and free will with respect to spirituality? The answer is essentially two-fold. First, if we have no free will, then how fair is it for a higher power to judge us for our actions? For this implies that not only is free will lacking, but for all intent and purposes, our lives are predetermined. Indeed, the whole of our life is foreordained. The entire world is therefore the result of some form of determinism. And if this is true, then as some forms of religion already believe, we have already been judged, "... all events of history, past, present, and future, have been already decided or are already known (by God, fate, or some other force), including human actions."[22]

Second, if we are created in the image of God, does that mean God is just as fallible as we are? If so, does God deserve to be worshipped? If this world is, with all of its evil, natural and manmade, so imperfect then on what grounds should we worship a creator that created so much misery, pain, hardship, and so forth?

Both of these issues are relevant when it comes to the question we are asking: "Is it irrational to believe in a higher power?"

# Part Two: Antithesis

## The Spiritual Edge: Rationality in Spirituality

*A man has free choice to the extent that he is rational.*
~ Thomas Aquinas

Well, our thesis side of this discussion certainly provided many reasons to discard and/or at the very least, doubt the notion of a god. Where some dissent to the information by those inclined to believe in a god has been noted as we traversed the agnostic/atheistic side of our discussion, there certainly has been no satisfactory logic or reason provided to believe. As such, it's time to embark on the antithesis to our thesis and determine if indeed it is irrational to believe in a god, a superior being, and if not—to discuss what then.

I believe there are many good reasons to believe in a higher power, and at least one of those reasons is rooted in what's known as practical reasoning. As we will see, practical reasoning insists that when in doubt, the best form of reasoning is outcome oriented. This is the pragmatic view: does it work?

# Chapter 6

# Why Are There Nonbelievers?

*Science without religion is lame,*
*religion without science is blind.*
~ Albert Einstein

There are many differences that research has uncovered when it comes to distinguishing between the brains of spiritual believers and nonbelievers. For example, numerous studies have demonstrated that "spiritual people have thicker brains and more active frontal lobes."[23] Other studies have been carried out to compare reasoning abilities between groups. This is usually done by using syllogisms to test logical thinking. One very interesting study shared by neuroscientist Dr. Andrew Newberg in his informative course, *The Spiritual Brain: Science and Religious Experience*, illustrates something common to both believers and unbelievers. In this study, both groups were provided with theistic and atheistic syllogisms. "Participants were asked to evaluate whether the syllogisms were internally consistent or not... The religious people did better on the pro-religious questions, and the non-religious persons did better on the anti-religious questions. The results suggest that both groups make logical mistakes, but they make them in the direction of their beliefs."[24]

## Neuroscience

Interestingly, a finding published in *Psychological Science* suggests that an awe-inspiring moment increases our tendency to believe in the supernatural.[25] This is something I found, too, when I conducted interviews with random people while traveling. Without exception, we found that those places in nature such as the jagged red cutouts and sharp, upward-pointed sandstone formations of Zion, Bryce, or the Grand Canyon always seemed to remind people of God and were often described as an outdoor citadel or temple—many described these kinds of surroundings as "God's church."

Are we wired to find causation and, in our lack of comprehension, do we opt for the supernatural? Note the researchers' comments regarding what they see as the irony to this finding.

"Many historical accounts of religious epiphanies and revelations seem to involve the experience of being awestruck by the beauty, strength, or size of a divine being, and these experiences change the way people understand and think about the world," says psychological scientist Piercarlo Valdesolo of Claremont McKenna College.

"We wanted to test the exact opposite prediction: It's not that the presence of the supernatural elicits awe, it's that awe elicits the perception of the presence of the supernatural."

Valdesolo and his colleague Jesse Graham of the University of Southern California tested this prediction by having participants watch awe-inspiring scenes from BBC's *Planet Earth* documentary series or neutral video clips from a news interview. Afterward, the participants were asked how much awe they felt while watching the video and whether they believed that worldly events unfold according to some god's or other non-human entity's plan.

"Overall, participants who had watched the awe-inspiring video tended to believe more in supernatural control and were more likely to believe in God when compared with the news-watching group. This effect held even when awe-inspiring but impossible scenes, such as a massive waterfall through city streets, were presented."

Another study showed that participants who watched the awe-inspiring clips became increasingly intolerant of uncertainty. This particular mindset—a discomfort with uncertainty—may explain why feelings of awe produce a greater belief in the supernatural.

"The irony in this is that gazing upon things that we know to be formed by natural causes, such as the jaw-dropping expanse of the Grand Canyon, pushes us to explain them as the product of supernatural causes," Valdesolo notes.[26]

In still another study reported by Newberg, nonbelievers and believers were shown distorted photos containing both real and non-real elements. "Believers were more likely to see things that were there, but sometimes they saw things that weren't there. Nonbelievers never saw things that weren't there, but sometimes they missed things that were there. Again, each group made mistakes, but they made them in the directions that were consistent with their beliefs."[27]

Newberg adds, "Another interesting result of this study is that when nonbelievers were given dopamine, their results were more similar to the results of the believers."[28] So, is belief a chemical reaction? Does a theist produce more dopamine than an atheist? When my wife proofed this book and came to this part, she commented, "Sounds a bit like my own reaction when I went on bio-identical hormone therapy—I felt the old spirituality assert itself again."

This begs the question, which came first? Do higher levels of dopamine increase our spiritual inclination? Is the brain thicker in believers because they are believers, or are they believers because the brain is thicker? Likewise, is the frontal lobe more active due to religious belief and/or practice, or was it more active to begin with and therefore that is why one is more likely to be a believer?

What else can neuroscience teach us about spirituality and the brain? Dean Hamer tells us in his book, *The God Gene*, that there is a gene in common to believers. Using the DNA and personality information from over 1,000 subjects, Hamer found a correlation between this gene and feelings of self-transcendence, or the idea that there is something larger than the individual. Hamer is careful to point out that this gene is not the only factor behind the predisposition of believers, but he does think that it is somehow involved.[29] However, not everyone agrees.

Writing in *Scientific America*, Carl Zimmer had this to say about Hamer's claims:

The role that genes play in religion is a fascinating question that's ripe for the asking. Psychologists, neurologists, and even evolutionary biologists have offered insights about how spiritual behaviors and beliefs emerge from the brain. It is reasonable to ask, as Hamer does, whether certain genes play a significant role in faith. But he is a long way from providing an answer.

Hamer, a geneticist at the National Cancer Institute, wound up on his quest for the God gene by a roundabout route. Initially he and his colleagues set out to find genes that may make people prone to cigarette addiction. They studied hundreds of pairs of siblings, comparing how strongly their shared heredity influenced different aspects of their personality. In addition to having their subjects fill out psychological questionnaires, the researchers also took samples of DNA from some of them. Hamer then realized that this database might let him investigate the genetics of spirituality.

He embarked on this new search by looking at the results of certain survey questions that measured a personality trait known as self-transcendence, originally identified by Washington University psychiatrist Robert Cloninger.

Cloninger found that spiritual people tend to share a set of characteristics, such as feeling connected to the world and a willingness to accept things that cannot be objectively demonstrated. Analyzing the cigarette study, Hamer confirmed what earlier studies had found: heredity is partly responsible for whether a person is self-transcendent or not. He then looked at the DNA samples of some of his subjects, hoping to find variants of genes that tended to turn up in self-transcendent people.

His search led him to a gene known as VMAT2. Two different versions of this gene exist, differing only at a single position. People with one version of the gene tend to score a little higher on self-transcendence tests. Although the influence is small, it is, Hamer claims, consistent. About half the people in the study had at least one copy of the self-transcendence-boosting version of VMAT2, which Hamer dubs the God gene.

Is the God gene real? The only evidence we have to go on at the moment is what Hamer presents in his book.[30]

Even with Zimmer's question about the God gene, it appears that there are some real differences between believers and nonbelievers. According to neuroscientist, Dr. Andrew Newberg, "The differences are manifested in how they think about and interpret reality. However, the differences are also reflected in the brain. Different parts of the brain react differently in believers and nonbelievers."[31]

## Ritual

There has been much debate among scholars regarding the definition of a ritual. However, there are some common denominators with rituals; when repeated in patterns, rhythmically, they directly affect the brain. Great orators know that getting the crowds involved, chanting, waving from side to side with their body motion, even holding hands, tends to unite the group and form not only deeper bonds among each other but greater loyalty toward the speaker. Whether it is the soapbox agitator sort, such as Adolf Hitler, or the religious zealot the likes of Jim Jones, the use of ritualistic behavior cements the faithfulness, even obedience of followers.

Structuring rituals so that they become regular and ordered further facilitates the effect. Doing the same thing over and over is one way of creating a ritual. Many successful politicians use this concept with their repeated use of slogans. Getting the audience to chant back the same slogans is a sign of a good political rally. Finding a way to get the audience to move rhythmically at the same time simply enhances their commitment.

Indeed, the rhythmic motion of the body affects everything from heart rate to brain rhythms. These external rhythms, whether musical in nature or the simple rocking of the body from side to side, can actually synchronize the body to the cadence.[32] Data shows that two people lying in bed next to each other can experience their breathing and heart rates coming together, synchronizing both like pendulum clocks all ticking to the same beat. Further, since our emotions are tied to our thoughts, our cognitive process notes the "togetherness" and reinforces the bond.

As for the brain, research with frequency following responses or FFRs have demonstrated clearly that the brain can be entrained, even slowing brain wave activity into the realms associated with a hypnotized subject. Newberg puts it this way, "The physiology of ritual is based on the rhythms synchronizing the brain so that it begins to actually diminish the usual flow of sensory information entering the brain."[33]

Newberg also points out that the parietal lobe decreases in activity during ritual. That may be important since it is this area of the brain that largely distinguishes self, space, and time. Some research has shown that this same area of the brain becomes less active during deep religious practices where one experiences a sense of oneness with all. Obviously, the sense of self, or the loss of the sense of self as separate, is often reported as accompanying the deep religious experience.

Rituals are part of the human experience. We all have our own rituals. It may be the order of events that we carry out every day when we get out of bed, and it may be our Sunday worship practice, but we all participate in rituals.

Now add to this the fact that we all have what neuroscience refers to as "mirror neurons," or neurons that exist for the sole purpose of mirroring the behavior of others. Just watching a person scratch themselves causes a mirror neuron to imitate the behavior, at least in our mind. This mirroring factor underlies much of the success behind neurolinguistic programming (NLP). So, what we have is a recipe for belief—belief in what is the only question. As such, we must recognize our vulnerabilities, and in doing so, be willing to question what we believe as well as entertain the why behind the what.

One of the dangers inherent to rituals has to do with their effect on groups. Research shows that groups that identify with each other as a result of a common ritual, say the annual visit to Mecca, form in-groups and therefore out-groups in their mind. That is, they judge the in-group more favorably and are less hostile toward it than to the out-group. For the psychology student, is this not reminiscent of the fiction work, *Lord of the Flies*? Its effect is the same. This sort of identification led to the tragedy in Rwanda. That said, in Newberg's words, "Ritual [itself] is a morally neutral technology."[34]

The rhythm involved in certain rituals should not be taken for granted. You feel rhythm within your body, but it drives your brain. "As it drives your body and brain, the rhythmic activity drives the hypothalamus and ultimately, your amygdala to generate emotional responses."[35] Obviously, the limbic system and the autonomic nervous system also become involved, making the ritual experience as close to a religious experience as one can imagine.

Various religious activities certainly employ ritual and rhythm. This tends to act not only as a cohesive bond with groups but as an emotional anchor that ties our memories to religious beliefs. Arguably, Christmas is one such ritual and the story of Christ combines with the music and a general sense of love to reinforce a belief in Christ.

There are a number of other interesting correlations between the brain and spiritual or religious practices. If you're interested in pursuing this further, I urge you to study Dr. Andrew Newberg's, *The Spiritual Brain: Science and Religious Experience*, a *Great Courses* presentation available on DVD and/or as an online course.

So, what appears to be the hardwiring in our brains that predisposes us to believe in the supernatural arguably is the result of some evolutionary mechanism. As discussed earlier, Dean Hamer is convinced that the so-called "God gene" is evidence of that possibility. Since the overwhelming majority of people throughout history have and continue to believe in a god, evolution may have crafted us that way in order to cope with the foreknowledge of death or to just get us through difficult times by providing means to diffuse stress and see beyond the fears of disease and uncertainty in life.[36]

Those like Richard Dawkins, the British evolutionary biologist, recognize this possible inheritable characteristic and its evolutionary nature as an artifact of the uninformed ages of the past. In Dawkins' opinion:

There is no reason for believing that any sort of gods exist, and quite good reason for believing that they do not exist and never have. It has all been a gigantic waste of time and a waste of life. It would be a joke of cosmic proportions if it weren't so tragic.[37]

Dr. Francis S. Collins, head of the Human Genome Project and one of the world's leading scientists, sees it differently. From his book, *The Language of God*, Collins is credited as being the man who "... has heard every argument against faith from scientists, and he can refute them. He has also heard the needless rejection of scientific truths by some people of faith, and he can counter that, too." Collins quite eloquently presents evidence for the belief in God, so we're left with differing opinions, but this much is certain—the brain is wired for religious experience. Is this so because the Creator wanted us to remember who we are, or is this so because the species needed an evolutionary advantage for survival?

There is an irony in all of this, and it comes down to the fact that the brain is made in such a way as to fit our religious experience, or in the alternative, our experience fits the brain. If I were to suggest that when a meditator focuses on a prayer that the language center in the brain becomes active, that would surprise no one. If I suggested that a meditation involving a visualization process elicited activity in the visual cortex, that too, would come as no surprise. So why should it surprise us to discover that feelings of unity and oneness arise when activity in the parietal lobe is diminished or that activity in the frontal lobe increases during focused meditation? In other words, for every experience there is an answer that is biological. What does that tell us?

## Religious Practices and the Brain

The word God is interesting, for perhaps more than any other word in any language, it stands out as potentially involving a greater number of meanings and emotional responses than all others. For some the word invokes hope, love, and peace, and for others it is a reference to nonsense, superstition, mental weakness, and for still more, the word elicits fear, anger, and even hatred. The ways we understand God inherently give rise to the meaning of God!

For spiritual and religious people, it is this personal understanding of God that forms the basis for the meaning and purpose in their lives. Indeed, the meaning in life is generally derived directly from our opinion of an afterlife—either you only go around once or there is much more to life than meets the eye.

Now, an interesting enquiry of late has been carried out by several different neuroscientists in a variety of experimental settings. It involves the use of sophisticated technology for evaluating changes in the brain due to religious and spiritual practices. Here's a really interesting study carried out by Dr. Andrew Newberg and his team. What they did was borrow a popular meditation technique from the tradition of Kundalini Yoga, known as Kirtan Kriya. This technique was secularized by informing participants that they were to make these sounds in a repeated fashion in order to assist in self-training a valued meditation practice. The subjects were older volunteers, and the preferred subject was someone who had experienced occasional memory loss—that typically associated with aging. They divided subjects into two groups. One group was told to listen to music for twelve minutes a day for eight weeks. The other group was told to repeat these sounds: sa-ta-na-ma. They were to say them aloud for two minutes, then whisper them for two minutes, then repeat them silently for four minutes, and then whisper them for two minutes and finally to speak them aloud for the final two minutes. Now they were to make finger movements as well while repeating the sounds. So, they would begin by touching their forefinger to their thumb when saying *sa*, and then their middle finger with *ta*, and the ring finger with *na* and so forth.

Twelve weeks later their brain scans were compared with their pre-test and with the music group. There was no change for those listening to music but some pretty substantial changes for those who practiced this meditation exercise. Now again, this exercise is considered by at least one spiritual teacher to be the exercise you should learn if you only learn one, but the group being studied did not have this knowledge. The *sa-ta-na-ma* is a mantra, and the finger movement is known as a mudra, but the experimental group did not know that they were actually employing an important religious practice; to them this was a secular exercise with simple sounds to assist in focusing on developing a meditation practice.

So, what were the findings? The experimental group showed great increases in activity in the frontal lobe, and these changes endured over time. The frontal lobe is, of course, what we use for focused attention. They also found significant differences in the thalamus. The thalamus has two sides, and initially the subjects showed activity in one side, but following the experiment, the subjects' thalamic activity had shifted to the opposite side, suggesting that somehow this exercise had fundamentally rewired the way the brain operated. Now the subjects were also given a number of psychological tests, including tests for verbal memory, visual attention, and task switching. The subjects in the experimental group once again showed significant improvement in all of these tests. Indeed, cognitively, the meditation group performed on average about ten percent better after the eight weeks of training. Not only that, but their experience of life changed as well. They became emotionally happier, experiencing fifteen to twenty percent less depression, anxiety, fear, and so forth. This finding implicates changes in the limbic system.[38]

So now, here's the question. To some religious people, the words: *sa-ta-na-ma* have meaning and power. As such, there are those who suggest that this experiment was not truly a secular experiment at all. For some, the words themselves invoked a special spiritual power due to their special spiritual significance. Now this is not uncommon where sacred languages are concerned. The sacred letter energies one encounters in

Kabbalah, for example, are considered to have not only meaning, but power. So, to utter the sound is to invoke a power or force of some kind. For the Babylonians the word "sesame" invoked a power derived from sesame oil. So, what would happen if you truly secularized this practice and used something like, do-ra, da, la or da-la-ra-do?

And one more thing—if you can truly gain this level of change in the brain through this one activity, carried out purportedly as a secular activity, what kind of changes could you get if deep religious practices of this kind were done daily for years? Is this the way the Tibetan monks gain so much control over their bodies?

The next time you feel that life is going by, and everything is same old same old, try meditation and see how your own brain changes. That said, we are nevertheless addressing the organ brain, and the question again might be, does the organ brain produce the spiritual experience or is there something beyond the organ brain that is involved in the spiritual experience—another chicken-and-egg sort of question?

Remember, we are still interrogating the "what and why" behind whether it is reasonable to believe in a higher power. I believe that one can see why so many people, especially our younger generation, can have a problem believing in anything other than the mechanistic reductionism found in scientism today. I have spoken to many scholars who readily admit that their peers are more likely **not** to take their work seriously if they are believers in some superpower, some afterlife. Indeed, in a conversation I enjoyed with Ralph Lewis, MD, Lewis admitted that he was willing to be uncertain about everything except his science and atheism. That said, he referred to himself as a "pragmatic atheist" when asked about how he treated his patients who did hold strong spiritual beliefs. As such, if you were one of his patients and you believed in a higher power, then as an informed medical doctor, Lewis would not challenge your beliefs and thereby rob you of your special sense of hope.

# Chapter 7

# Religion or Psychology

*A young man who wishes to remain a sound atheist cannot be too careful of his reading.*
~ C.S. Lewis

Religion and spirituality offer us hope. When we lose a loved one, there is hope that we will once again be with them. There is hope that they continue to go on somewhere, in some other dimension. When we are our most fearful, there is hope that we are being looked after, that there is some purpose and protection to all that we might endure. Deep down in all of us, there is the certain realization that we are mortal, and our lives could abruptly end at any moment, and religious/spiritual practices help us to go on with some certainty that even when the death of the body occurs, it's not really our death—our complete end or annihilation.

Religious and spiritual practices have provided a moral code and asked the highest of us. In the name of religion, many have devoted their lives to helping others. Religious charities have rehabilitated and saved many lives. Religion has contributed incredible art, music, and science. Religious doctrines in general preach altruism. It is true, religion has been used as a pretext for many historical travesties, but so has the notion of justice. Think of the violence the interpretation of "justice" has caused. The world sees something deemed unjust; sometimes the so-called unjust actions have actually been nothing more than propaganda promulgated for purposes of hidden agendas, and in the name of "unjust," nations rise up against each other and send their children to be mutilated and killed. Does this mean that we should throw out the notion of justice?

# Truth

The matter is much more complex than many would like to think. However, when religions vilify each other and claim to have the only *truth*, they open the doors to criticism that their truth is nothing more than club nonsense designed to create members and collect dues. So, if there is a real downside to religion and spirituality, it arises out of their exclusive assertions and arrogations. But how is this different from any club rivalry? All clubs, including the club of nations, promote a form of centrism. In a very real sense, there is little difference between the rivalry and competition that exists in clubs such as the NFL than in any other club except for how the rivalry is acted out.

It is wise when you examine the legacy of religious or spiritual practices to consider the leaders, their motives, soundness of mind, and those who followed them as opposed to the flag they waved. Germany is a great nation with wonderful people despite their role in two world wars. The people followed a leader, sometimes willingly brainwashed and sometimes as the result of coercion, and how is that different than your own centrism under the same pressures?

Systemic to the human condition is the willingness by all to ignore the obvious and sometimes at our own peril. I have long thought of this human propensity as the *Principle of Psychological Exception*. This principle simply translates to how one excludes themselves from known dangers. Take the cigarette smoker, for example — the data is clear and yet for most people who smoke, they are the exception. The warnings apply to others, not to them. They will not find themselves needing an artificial voice box, an oxygen source as a permanent part of their wardrobe, a scar down the center of their chest from having their ribs separated so their heart could be bypassed during surgery, and so forth. No — for each of these smokers, they are the exception.

## Willful Blindness

Now add to this the construct known as *Willful Blindness* and you have the mixture necessary to explain how it is so easy for the herd animal, humans, to follow the Pied Piper and remain blissfully unaware of the inherent dangers in doing so.

There is a wonderful true example of willful blindness provided by Margaret Heffernan in her book by the same name. The story is of a woman in Libby, Montana, Gayla Benefield, who discovered an alarming death rate and, after some research, linked it to the vermiculite mined there, which actually contained some asbestos. Despite her evidence and the fact that the death rate was eighty times greater in Libby than elsewhere in America, the citizens of Libby by and large ignored or ridiculed her. Some of the people in Libby actually made up bumper stickers stating, "Yes, I'm from Libby, Montana. No, I don't have asbestosis." Finally, the government got involved and verified the asbestosis problem and the death rate relationship.[39]

Now it doesn't take a social scientist to find possible explanations for this behavior. Some in the town may have worried about what this kind of news would do to their property values, others may have been concerned that the damage to their business could bankrupt them, still others could simply be resisting change, while some may have refused to accept the idea because of the guilt they might feel due to raising their families in a place certain to doom them to an early death after a long painful suffering. Many more reasons as unique as each individual in Libby could well underlie their refusal to acknowledge the danger present in their community, but the fact is, that is exactly what most did!

So, is it religion that is the cause of the ignorance, the likes of which is discussed above, or is it the psychology of those who follow? What is it that you are willing to go along with in the name of justice? When is a whistleblower a traitor and when are they a hero? Do you really know the difference, or do you just go along with the popular notion of the moment?

Research shows us that even strong-willed confident people can be swayed to see what they don't see and come to conclusions that their senses tell them are false. Repeated studies have shown that if you take a subject—we'll say Mr. X— and place him with a group of others who are in on the research, that the group will invariably influence the judgment of Mr. X. We reviewed this earlier with the line length study. Soon Mr. X goes along with the group in identifying the shorter line as the longer line.

When history tells stories of atrocities such as the Christian Crusades and Holocaust, look not at Christianity or the German people per se, look first in the mirror! The behavior is not due to religion or justice or what have you; it is the result of mad leaders and blind followers. The notion of *sheeple* is gaining popularity today, but the theme and the psychology are certainly not new!

## Secularism

Now by contrast to blaming religion for the evils of the world, I would be remiss not to remind you that we have more and more leaders stepping out with the charge that much of the increase in incivility found everywhere in America is due to secularism. For example, quoting a CNN piece:

> Attorney General Bill Barr decried attacks on religious values in a speech Friday, tying a movement of "militant secularism" to societal maladies including the opioid epidemic and "an increase in senseless violence."
>
> ... Barr outlined a grim vision of cultural trends, saying a "moral upheaval" and decades of efforts to undermine religion had given way to growing illegitimacy rates, drug use, and "angry, alienated young males"—a population associated recently with a spate of domestic attacks...

"... Among the militant secularists are many so-called progressives. But where is the progress?" Barr asked. "Those who defy the creed risk a figurative burning at the stake: social, educational, and professional ostracism and exclusion waged through lawsuits and savage social media campaigns."[40]

It is worth noting here that there is a strong correlation between secularism and the goals of Marxism, socialism, and communism. Writing in *The Atlantic*, Ross Douthat begins his discussion on the issue by quoting Josh Muravchik:

Communists—or Marxists, doctrinaire socialists, dialectical materialists, whatever you want to call them. Here was a very tribal bunch. They were dedicated to the overthrow of religion and religious opiates. They protected themselves in tribal fashion in academia, government, and politics. They defined themselves largely by what they hated. Etc, etc. Indeed, it's worth remembering that both Marx and Engels came to their Communism via their atheism rather than the other way around.[41]

Whether secularism or religion are behind much of the troubles we face in today's world is something that may be debated for a very long time, but it is clear that the conflict between the two is not going away any day soon.

# Chapter 8

# Reason

*I'm generally a very pragmatic person:*
*that which works, works.*
~ Linus Torvalds

As we saw in Part One, there are very many people today, particularly our Gen X and Millennials, who simply find the idea of a belief in an afterlife or creator, a higher power, superstitious mumbo-jumbo. They argue, as do some of their older mentors, that spiritual beliefs are irrational. As Ayn Rand put it:

> The good, say the mystics of spirit, is God, a being whose only definition is that he is beyond man's power to conceive—a definition that invalidates man's consciousness and nullifies his concepts of existence... Man's mind, say the mystics of spirit, must be subordinated to the will of God... Man's standard of value, say the mystics of spirit, is the pleasure of God, whose standards are beyond man's power of comprehension and must be accepted on faith... The purpose of man's life... is to become an abject zombie who serves a purpose he does not know, for reasons he is not to question.[42]

Christopher Hitchens easily dismissed spirituality with this statement, "What can be asserted without evidence can also be dismissed without evidence."[43] Is it evidence we need to believe? If so, are there other criteria that we should also take into consideration? I mean there is no evidence per se that a higher power doesn't exist—or is there? Is reason the enemy of the religion?

It would seem that many believers are intentionally alienated from reasoning about their beliefs by some of their leaders. In the words of the sixteenth-century German priest Martin Luther, "Whoever wants to be a Christian should tear the eyes out of his reason." Or in the words of St. Ignatius Loyola, "We should always be disposed to believe that which appears to us to be white is really black, if the hierarchy of the church so decides."

Religious insistence on abandoning reason is possibly the number-one cause of religious rebellion. It's akin to insisting on magical beings whether they are creatures such as the Easter Bunny or the Unicorn. By arguing that reason has no place in our enquiry, religion disqualifies itself from the world of the rational. That said, not all spiritual systems or practices share the denial of reason. Even among the more classical systems such as Judaism, Catholicism, Buddhism, and more, there are those who ignore the edict insisting on the denial of rational processes. For these people, there is a more mystical meaning to the so-called literal teachings found in their doctrinal literature.

The formal process of the use of our faculties for ratiocination may actually argue that it is irrational to be an atheist. Why is that? Well, there are multiple reasons, including the formal nature of reason, something we'll examine in a few moments under the designations of theoretical and practical reasoning. However, for the moment, think about this. Quoting Dr. Eric Charles from his article "Atheism is Irrational", appearing in *Psychology Today,*

Atheism is demonstrably, certainly, and definitively irrational... If, by "atheism", you mean an assertion of absolute certainty that there is no God or gods; what my friend Peter would refer to as his "Gnostic Atheism". I don't know anyone who claims to be this form of atheist who would not agree that the final step to Gnosticism is at least a bit irrational.[44]

Charles goes on to clarify his thinking and to set agnosticism apart from atheism.

> While I am arguing against claims of absolute knowledge, I am not claiming that anyone should plead ignorance. While there are times when a person could rightly judge that there is insufficient evidence with which to form an opinion on some matter, this is not one of those times. William James tells us that we should be most concerned with forced, living, momentous decisions. Roughly speaking, these are decisions where it is difficult or impossible to be neutral, where there is a possibility of our going in either direction, and where the decision has genuine consequences for how we live our lives. In such situations, James argues, sitting on the fence is akin is denying the importance of the issue. Or, to put it another way, if the issue is indeed important, then *failing to make a choice might well be the least rational option available.*[45] (My emphasis added.)

When you think about atheism, or for that matter agnosticism, in this light, just how rational is it? Could it be that there exists a certain stubbornness among the deniers that might even be considered somewhat narcissistic? I mean, think about how many of these people seem to represent a pattern of self-centered, arrogant thinking and behavior, a lack of empathy and consideration for other people, and an excessive need for admiration. Isn't this the classical definition of a narcissist? Webster adds this: "Others often describe people with NPD [Narcissistic Personality Disorder] as cocky, manipulative, selfish, patronizing, and demanding."

Now in fairness, the religious zealot who arrogates exclusive truth and evangelizes everywhere they go may clearly fit the narcissist definition as well. My point is simple though; by contrast to those who search for meaning, those who believe they already know it all, whether atheist or religionist, may well be the very ones who miss the greater meaning in the enquiry about God.

So, is it irrational not to believe like physicist Marcelo Gleiser says? Quoting Gleiser from an article in *Scientific American*:

I honestly think atheism is inconsistent with the scientific method. What I mean by that is, what is atheism? It's a statement, a categorical statement that expresses belief in nonbelief. "I don't believe even though I have no evidence for or against. Simply I don't believe." Period. It's a declaration. But in science we don't really do declarations. We say, "Okay, you can have a hypothesis; you have to have some evidence against or for that." And so an agnostic would say, "Look, I have no evidence for God or any kind of god." (What god, first of all? The Maori gods or the Jewish or Christian or Muslim God? Which god is that?) But on the other hand, an agnostic would acknowledge no right to make a final statement about something he or she doesn't know about. "The absence of evidence is not evidence of absence," and all that. This positions me very much against all of the "New Atheist" guys—even though I want my message to be respectful of people's beliefs and reasoning, which might be community-based, or dignity-based, and so on. And I think obviously the Templeton Foundation likes all of this because this is part of an emerging conversation. It's not just me; it's also my colleague the astrophysicist Adam Frank and a bunch of others, talking more and more about the relation between science and spirituality.[46]

Let's then explore reason. There is a formal structure to the application of reason—so let's turn to it for some deeper insight.

## Regarding Science and Religion

There are essentially three positions available to the rational mind regarding science and religion. The first position might be stated this way: Science and religion are inherently in conflict. The second position may be stated this way: Science and religion are inherently not in conflict. The third position, and the one I will defend, can be stated this way: Science and religion are potentially in conflict.

So, according to the first position, science informs us of the world as it is, and religion instructs us in how God wants us to interpret the world. Science tells us the universe is many times older than the 6 to 7,000 years old as implied in the Bible. Science tells us that the Earth is not the center of the universe while for centuries Christians assumed the Earth was the center of the universe. In principle, it is not possible for science and religion to find agreement if for no other reason than the revealed word, as found in the sacred books, informs believers who, in order to demonstrate their commitment to God, must refrain from asking those questions that science regularly challenges regarding scripture. In other words, faith must triumph over reason. Indeed, reason is sinful. In the words of the sixteenth-century priest Martin Luther, "Reason is a whore, the greatest enemy that faith has; it never comes to the aid of spiritual things, but more frequently than not struggles against the divine Word, treating with contempt all that emanates from God."

Now the second position argues that science and religion are two different interpretations of the world and need not be at odds with each other. Science, according to the Harvard scholar Stephen Jay Gould, informs us of the realm of fact while religion instructs us in the realm of theory. Science is concerned with factual observations and empirical facts while religion is concerned with the purpose of the natural world. Further, both interpretations can be right and religious views sometimes end up trumping those of science. An example of this is the Steady

State theory popular in the twentieth century. The Steady State theory proposed that the "universe has no beginning or end in time, and from any point within it the view on the grand scale—i.e., the average density and arrangement of galaxies—is the same."[47] This theory did not sit well with religious people because it presupposed there was no act of creation and therefore no Creator. As it turned out, religious people were right and the Steady State fell away to the Big Bang theory, from nothing (no thing)—everything.

Now there are many problems with this second position, including so-called factual or historical statements made in religious scripture. So, when the Bible informs us that Moses was transfigured, that is a factual statement from a historical account. As such, it is indeed making an empirical statement about the world.

The third position, that of potential conflict, is more tenable to most thinkers. Many mystery schools and sacred text scholars see these sacred religious texts as teaching stories wrapped in metaphors. So, is it possible that there need not be tension between science and religion? This translates into an answer to the question, "What do we do when religion and science conflict?" and the answer is, "Look at it on a case-by-case basis." For the fact is, as Michael Murray, a senior visiting scholar in philosophy at Franklin and Marshall College in Lancaster, Pennsylvania, puts it, "So when you were in the process of doing, engaging in this sort of balancing act, a religious believer, when there's tension with a certain scientific claim, really faces four options. (1) To reject their religious belief. (2) To reject their interpretation of the religious data, to re-interpret how they understand and experience a text. (3) To reject the evidence of their senses. Or (4) to reject an interpretation of the sense data and reject the claim that science has understood the data correctly."[48]

It seems pretty clear that where a potential conflict may exist, it does so entirely due to how one interprets the sacred scripts. When Krishna instructs Arjuna that to be true to his duty, he must wage war against members of his family and his friends, the metaphor addresses the importance and meaning of duty. When Job is plagued, the metaphor speaks to how easy it is to abandon faith and God when things don't go your way, something often reported when a believer's expectation is disappointed. If these stories are teaching parables full of metaphors designed to address the way we live, then their literal interpretation is a moot point.

There are scientists today who refuse to accept the possibility that there is an afterlife or supernatural. These men and women are what we call members of scientism, for they have made their absolute belief a religious belief (that of science) in the sense that they are unable to prove what they hold dear to their central argument: there is no afterlife or supernatural anything.

There are also strict fundamentalists who believe their sacred texts to be the literal word of God and interpret their worldview accordingly. They deny science and hold dear to the words of men like Martin Luther who also stated, "Reason must be deluded, blinded, and destroyed. Faith must trample underfoot all reason, sense, and understanding, and whatever it sees must be put out of sight and... know nothing but the word of God."

I am of the opinion that the average reasonable person would find both extremes unreasonable. It seems more logical to accept the words of Albert Einstein: "Science can only ascertain what is, but not what should be, and outside of its domain, value judgments of all kinds remain necessary." And/or the words of Pope John Paul II: "Faith and reason are like two wings on which the human spirit rises to the contemplation of truth, and God has placed in the human heart a desire to know the truth—in a word, to know himself—so that, by knowing and loving God, men and women may also come to the fullness of truth about themselves."

## Two Kinds of Reason

All right, let's discuss reason and its two primary forms. Philosophically speaking, *practical reason* is the use of reason to decide *how to act*. It contrasts with *theoretical reason*, often called speculative reason, which is the use of reason to decide *what to follow*. Practical reason decides how the world *should be* and what individuals *should do*. Theoretical reason tries to assess the way things *are*.[49]

It is through theoretical reasoning that science operates. We come to know the world as a result of observation and formalize this knowledge as a result of verification. It is worth noting that theoretical reasoning may include probable inferences by way of some explanations of our universe. As such, some generally accepted theories, like the explanation for earthquakes being due to tectonic plates shifting, are considered reasonable forms of theoretical reasoning because they offer the best probable explanation.

That said, let's look at what the Big Bang theory asserts. At *no time* there was singularity. Singularity divided itself (bang), and from that we have everything. Further, despite its popularity, predictions arise from the theory that have not borne out. Additionally, other problems with the Big Bang theory include such facts as it violates the first law of thermodynamics and the law of entropy. It may be our best theory—but it is still only a theory. As a theory, it is, in fact, what the brilliant mathematician Kurt Gödel termed a *first principle*. And as Gödel demonstrated, all first principles are inherently unprovable.

Now another first principle might be similar to the genesis stories shared by many religions. So, in the beginning, there was only God, and God divided *itself*, creating all that is. Since first principles are unprovable, it would seem that using theoretical reasoning to interrogate them is somewhat futile. That said, you can definitely interrogate predictions made by this first principle, and those who attack religion often do. But attacking the notion that God is omnipotent is quite different from attacking the first principle itself—the idea that there is an Intelligence that is the creative force behind creation.

Now let's think about practical reasoning for a moment. Saint Thomas Aquinas considered the first principle of practical reason in his *Summa Theologiæ* to be good: "Good is to be done and pursued, and evil is to be avoided." Let's think about good for a moment. I think we all can agree that to be happy and healthy is good. I think we'd all also agree that improved cognitive abilities are good, and so is the sense of well-being. Most of us would also agree that added longevity is good, for as the old story goes, "Ask a 99-year-old if they want to live to be 100, and they'll most certainly answer in the affirmative."

Practical reasoning then has to do with how we live and what we choose to do. If I feel poorly, do I go to the doctor? If I go, I will lose a day's pay, but if I don't, I may get worse and lose a week's pay as a result of being out ill. I must make a decision, and this decision is based on practical reasoning. In other words, theoretical reasoning may give rise to advances in science while practical reasoning instructs my day-to-day life decisions.

So, to that end, in the next chapter we'll examine the issue of quality of life and its relationship to living a spiritual life versus a non-spiritual life. For the question is: Are we compelled on the basis of practical reasoning to rationally choose a spiritual path over an atheistic or agnostic one? In other words, will I live longer and be healthier and happier if I choose religiosity of some form over the secular mechanistic view? If so, it seems that the wisest and therefore most reasonable choice would be to choose spirituality. And if this is true, then the decision is at least based on practical reason, and ergo, it cannot be deemed to be irrational or unreasonable. So, let's just see what the evidence has to say.

# Chapter 9

# Well-Being

*So never lose an opportunity of urging a practical beginning, however small, for it is wonderful how often in such matters the mustard-seed germinates and roots itself.*
~ Florence Nightingale

Practical decisions are generally made on the basis of personal gain. Well-being, a sound mind and body, are certainly considered to be advantageous over their alternatives. So, what character traits are indicative of well-being? In 2004 Martin Seligman and Christopher Peterson published their findings regarding character in their book, *Character Strengths and Virtues.* According to the authors, there are six classes of virtues that are made up of twenty-four character strengths. In a recent study, cognitive scientist Scott Barry Kaufman, together with Spencer Greenberg, Susan Cain, and others, collected data on 517 people looking for a correlation between character as described by Seligman and Petersen, and well-being. They found hope to be the top trait correlated with well-being.[50]

There has been much research done on the effects of hopelessness and helplessness, and it is worth looking at this now. However, I should warn you, some people may find the following reports of experiments upsetting and disturbing. Today, such research would be met with great resistance from activists and the general public, and hopefully would not be allowed. However, just because we find the research methods abhorrent does not mean we should simply forget the information that has already been learned from them.

## Helplessness/Hopelessness

In 1970, Martin Seligman and Dennis Groves reported on research that demonstrated learned helplessness. In this research, electrical shocks were delivered to dogs who could not escape. Later, the dogs were provided with a safe area, an area they could escape to, but instead of escaping, they just lay there hopelessly and took the shock. In other words, the dogs had learned they were helpless; indeed, they had learned it so well that they no longer tried to escape. Further, the conditioned animals' immune systems were weakened and their will to live diminished.[51]

In 1957, Curt Richter forced rats to swim in an acrylic glass cylinder filled with water and from which they could not escape. Using both domestic and wild rats, Richter discovered that recently trapped wild rats drowned very quickly. Some simply swam to the bottom of the bucket, rammed a few times against the walls, and never came up again. They apparently accepted their situation as hopeless and drowned very quickly. Domestic rats did somewhat better, but they, too, drowned in no more than fifteen minutes. However, when Richter rescued the rat and held it in his hand for a few moments, dried it off, and gave it a rest before returning it to the water, the rats could swim for up to sixty hours before drowning. The hand of hope held out an apparent promise of rescue and that provided the energy of hope.[52]

## Energy of Hope

Hope is a powerful force. Repeated studies with animals, as gross as many of them are, have demonstrated that learned helplessness is a death sentence. This death sentence may well explain the many human deaths that follow when a person believes their life is without hope. Some people have been known to just lie down and die for no medical reason. In one study carried out by Stephen L. Stern, MD, of the department of psychiatry at the University of Texas Health Science Center at San Antonio, the death rate among the hopeless was almost three times higher than for the hopeful. Quoting for a moment, "... significantly more hopeless study participants died than hopeful participants. Specifically, twenty-nine percent of the hopeless participants died, compared with eleven percent of the hopeful participants."[53] Additionally, PubMed reports on a large-scale NIH sponsored study involving 2,428 men with this conclusion: "Our findings indicate that hopelessness is a strong predictor of adverse health outcomes, independent of depression and traditional risk factors."[54]

Hopelessness and helplessness often follow tragic events like the Twin Towers, or natural catastrophes like tsunamis and hurricanes. Hopelessness can lead to serious forms of depression including persistent suicidal ideation. Many studies have shown that depression increases mortality risk. Indeed, longitudinal studies have demonstrated that: "The association between depression and mortality persists over long periods of time and has emerged among women in recent decades, despite contemporaneous improvements in the treatment of depression and reduction of stigma associated with depression."[55]

The idea of a higher power, a purpose to life, provides tremendous strength and support through the mechanism of hope. Quoting the abstract of R.L. Sevensky from a paper titled "Religion and Illness: An Outline of Their Relationship":

Religion serves at least three functions for the sick or dying patient. (1) It provides a theoretical framework in which to make sense of illness and mortality by understanding them as punishment, education, purification, sacrifice, or mystery, and it does so without denying the reality of these experiences. (2) It provides such practical resources for coping with sickness, suffering, and mortality as prayer, social support, and ritual actions aimed at forgiveness, transcendence, and healing. (3) It gives hope in the face of inevitable death.[56]

## Gratitude

The second highest character trait correlated with well-being is gratitude. The gratitude attitude is all-important when it comes to engendering a strong immune and endocrine system. I have suggested on many occasions that we should all begin our day with a smile and a thank you. If you try this for yourself, you will notice the difference very quickly. Smiling fools the brain and it releases those good feeling neurochemicals, endorphins, and the thank you turns your focus toward the positive aspects of life, encouraging well-being. A popular article by Courtney Smith appearing in *Visible Body* explains the mechanics involved:

The muscles of expression located around the mouth are the depressor anguli oris, therisorius, the zygomaticus major, the zygomaticus minor, and the levator labii superioris. All of these muscles, specifically the zygomaticus muscles, are involved with smiling; they pull the orbicularis oris (the circular muscle of your mouth) upwards. These muscles are innervated by the various branches of the facial nerve (VII), which—when the muscles are activated—send signals to the brain that you are smiling.

From there, endorphins are released into the bloodstream from the pituitary gland and the brain and spinal cord from the hypothalamus. Endorphins are opioid (chemicals that bind to opiate receptors) peptides that act as neurotransmitters. Think of endorphins as the body's natural painkillers, or opiates; they are released in times of stress (good and bad), exercise, excitement, pain, love, and other emotional states, and you feel awesome because of them. If you've ever smiled helplessly at a picture of a puppy or kitten, you're feeling the effects of endorphins.[57]

Additionally, another study at the University of Kansas demonstrated the influence of a fake smile. "... Researchers had subjects use chopsticks to shape their mouths into smiles or frowns, and then induce a stressful situation. The results were surprising: those simulating smiles had lower heart rates and stress levels than those faking frowns."[58]

In a study carried out by Joel Wong and Joshua Brown published by the Greater Good Science Center at UC Berkeley, researchers found that gratitude improved mental health. "Compared with the participants who wrote about negative experiences or only received counseling, those who wrote gratitude letters reported significantly better mental health four weeks and twelve weeks after their writing exercise ended. This suggests that gratitude writing can be beneficial not just for healthy, well-adjusted individuals, but also for those who struggle with mental health concerns."[59]

Gratitude has also been shown to literally alter the molecular structure of the brain and the human heart. According to a UCLA's Mindfulness Awareness Research Center study, "Having an attitude of gratitude can change the molecular structure of your brain, keeping gray matter functioning properly, and it can make us healthier and happier."[60]

Gratitude for life is another essential feature implicit in spirituality. Indeed, gratitude may be the ultimate spiritual practice. Eric Demeter puts it this way, "Here's a theological sequence that is paramount to understanding this: gratitude begets humility, which begets God's grace... Gratitude has been called the 'gateway' spiritual discipline. As Psalm 100:4 commands us, 'Enter His gates with thanksgiving and His courts with praise; give thanks to Him and praise His name.' In gratitude, we thank God not just for the stuff that fills our storage spaces, but for Him."[61]

## Love

The third highest character strength positively correlated with well-being is love. Love is more than a powerful character trait influencing our well-being, it is the essence of spiritual practice. "Jesus said unto him, Thou shalt love the Lord thy God with all thy heart, and with all thy soul, and with all thy mind. This is the first and great commandment. And the second is like unto it, Thou shalt love thy neighbor as thyself. On these two commandments hang all the law and the prophets."

Certainly, love is not limited to the practice of spirituality for even the atheist can love his neighbor and many do. Still, where spiritual practices are concerned, the notion of unconditional love rises above what most think of as the practice of brotherly love. Forgiveness is considered by most spiritually minded people to be absolutely necessary if we ourselves are ever to be forgiven for our own missteps. It is therefore not uncommon to witness the spiritually oriented victim forgive the perpetrator of the most heinous of crimes against them.

The most primary relationship when it comes to spiritual love is the necessity to love thyself. If we are unable to love ourselves, then we are unable to love our neighbor. Learning to love ourselves is therefore a part and parcel of the spiritual path. The old admonishment paraphrased, "Love yourself and then find something larger than yourself to love," is not only healthy in a pragmatic sense, but also spiritual in the larger scheme.

As such, the three most important characteristics indicative of well-being are the same three most promoted by a spiritual life. Exactly how does this flesh out when it comes to the relative health of the believer versus the nonbeliever? This is something we'll look at in the next chapter, but first a sidebar. One of my readers of the manuscript said this to me: "Okay, I get it. You might be happier and healthier if you believe, and I accept that it is not irrational to believe, but how is that enough in and of itself to make this sort of commitment? I mean, is this supposed to represent reasons to believe because I don't think it does."

My answer had two parts that I'll share with you now, getting a little ahead of myself. First, this work is not about proving that God exists, but rather that, contrary to the arguments of many, it is not *irrational* or unreasonable to believe in a higher power or life after death! *That is indeed the single most important objective motivating the writing of this book.* Second, we all make choices in life. The synthesis of the information contained herein is up to every reader. If you choose to be an unbeliever, that certainly is your choice. I am not here to sell you religiosity per se. Just as with the way I used practical reasoning with the doctor visit, you are solely responsible and fully empowered to make your own choice. Perhaps we don't need to be religious or spiritual to take advantage of much of the well-being research spelled out in this chapter. After all, one can be grateful and hopeful without believing in a higher power, so maybe, just maybe, the question is, can you gain as much without a belief in a life after death or some form of spiritual connectedness?

It may be worth thinking about spirituality for a moment in order to qualify the opportunities suggested by way of the connection to a better life, including overall health as will be discussed in the next chapter. So, what does it mean to be spiritual? Quoting from an article appearing in *Very Well Mind* and titled "What is Spirituality?"

Spirituality is not a single path or belief system. There are many ways to experience spirituality and the benefits of a spiritual experience. For some people, this might involve the belief in a higher power or a specific religious practice.

For others, it may involve experiencing a sense of connection to a higher state or a sense of inter-connectedness with the rest of humanity and nature. Some signs of spirituality can include:

- Asking deep questions about topics such as suffering and what happens after death
- Deepening connections with other people
- Experiencing compassion and empathy for others
- Experiencing feelings of interconnectedness
- Feelings of awe and wonder
- Seeking happiness beyond material possessions or other external rewards
- Seeking meaning and purpose
- Wanting to make the world a better place.[62]

Obviously, this description indicates that one may be spiritual and still have reservations about believing in a higher power.

## Chapter 10

# Health

*At the end of the day, the quality of life is all we have.*

~ John Mackey

Following on the idea of the benefits obtained from having a spiritual perspective, it becomes incumbent upon us to examine in more detail the quality of life experienced between groups—believers versus nonbelievers. According to Emma Seppälä, Science Director of the Center for Compassion and Altruism Research and Education at Stanford University and Co-Director of the Yale College Emotional Intelligence Project at Yale University, "Whether you consider yourself Christian, Buddhist, or mindful spiritual yogi, [data] suggests you are more likely to report being *very happy*, have a longer life, have a lower risk of depression and suicide, be more resilient, be more faithful in relationships, have happier children, and be more satisfied with your family life."[63] Seppälä explains that this happens because the believer is more likely to meditate to cope with stress, more likely to have a built-in community that supports them, more likely to volunteer or donate and thereby lend purpose and meaning to their lives, and more likely to turn to prayer and have hope. Indeed, quoting again, "Research suggests prayer helps people find comfort by helping them deal with difficult emotions, encourages forgiveness, and leads to healthier relationships."[64]

## Forgiveness

A study conducted by Frank D. Fincham, scholar and director of the Florida State University Family Institute, argues, "Prayer can lead to cooperation, forgiveness in relationships."[65] Shane

Sharp, a graduate student studying sociology at UW-Madison, found that prayer can help people handle difficult emotions.[66] Another study carried out by Florida State University psychologist Nathaniel Lambert, revealed that prayer increases forgiveness. Quoting *Science Daily*, "... One single prayer can cause a striking difference in feelings." They also discovered that prayer over time had a powerful positive influence on relationships.[67]

How does this common spiritual practice exert its healing effects? The psychological scientists have an idea: Most of the time, couples profess and believe in shared goals, but when they hit a rough patch, they often switch to adversarial goals like retribution and resentment. These adversarial goals shift cognitive focus to the self, and it can be tough to shake that self-focus. Prayer appears to shift attention from the self back to others, which allows the resentments to fade.[68]

## Health

Further, as a believer, you are less likely to visit the doctor as often, have greater feelings of well-being, and fear death less than the nonbeliever.[69] Additionally, the research reveals these extra benefits: "Better health; less hypertension; less stress, even during difficult times; more positive feelings; less depression; greater psychological well-being; [and] superior ability to handle stress."[70]

In an interesting study designed to reverse engineer longevity, researchers discovered that all but 5 of 263 centenarians interviewed belonged to some faith-based community.[71]

Here are some more truly interesting scientific findings regarding religion and spirituality:

- Helps resist junk food
- Puts a smile on your face, and that releases endorphins

- Raises healthy self-esteem
- Soothes anxiety
- Protects against depression
- Motivates regular checkups and better health care
- Lowers blood pressure[72]

A Harvard study showed that the positive-based emotions attached to religious and spiritual practices safeguard against the effects of negative emotions.[73]

Vast scientific literature has detailed how negative emotions harm the body. For example, serious sustained stress or fear can alter biological systems in a way that, over time, adds up to "wear and tear" and, eventually, illnesses such as heart disease, stroke, and diabetes. Chronic anger and anxiety can disrupt cardiac function by changing the heart's electrical stability, hastening atherosclerosis, and increasing systemic inflammation.

Jack P. Shonkoff, Julius B. Richmond FAMRI Professor of Child Health and Development at HSPH and at the Harvard Graduate School of Education, and Professor of Pediatrics at Harvard Medical School, explains that early childhood "toxic stress" — the sustained activation of the body's stress response system resulting from such early life experiences as chronic neglect, exposure to violence, or living alone with a parent suffering severe mental illness — has harmful effects on the brain and other organ systems. Among these effects is a hair-trigger physiological response to stress, which can lead to a faster heart rate, higher blood pressure, and a jump in stress hormones.[74]

Bottom line, there is a real pragmatic application here. If you're healthier, happier, and live longer — why would you not risk believing? Is it really more rational to dismiss the unproven possibility that there may be a higher power in favor of the unproven possibility that there isn't? What do you think a truly rational person is likely to choose and, as importantly, why?

## Chapter 11

# Our Need to Understand

*Join me in my quest for a greater understanding of our existence.*
*Join me in my desire for a greater self.*
*Join me as I seek the humility to*
*love and understand my fellow man.*
~ Bryant H. McGill

The social psychologist Erich Fromm suggested that religion serves to provide a stable reference over time. People need that reference in order to subdue what might otherwise arise and has been termed "ontological anxiety." Andrew Newberg shares a story in his *Spiritual Brain* course that illustrates this need. Paraphrased, it seems there was a medical doctor practicing in Africa. A patient came to him due to a mosquito bite that caused malaria. The physician treated him with antibiotics. A few days later the physician saw the patient coming out of the local shaman's shack, so he asked the patient, "Why are you seeing the shaman? He only deals in spiritual matters. I provided your medical treatment. If you didn't believe in medicine, why did you come to me?" The patient responded, "I came to you because I was bitten by a mosquito. I visited my shaman to find out why!"[75]

Human beings have a need to understand the world. We need to believe there are reasons. We search for causes, and we tend to think that there is a purpose behind most everything. Indeed, our brains are wired to process information in precisely this manner.

## Causal Relationships

Think of it this way, some 3,000 years ago in the Savanna, if we were to hear a noise in the bushes behind us, we would have to decide the cause. If it were a man-eating beast and we failed to associate a possible cause behind the noise that included a man-eater, then we were lunch, and our genes were not passed on. The simple fact is, our brain is a believing machine; we would not have survived if it were otherwise. We build causal relationships out of everything, and we believe the information we build, and again, if our ancestors failed to do this, they simply would not have passed on their genes, and we wouldn't be here.

Because we are hardwired in this and other ways, does that mean we should, as some insist, abandon our spiritual and religious beliefs since they arise only as a result of some Darwinian selection process? Now that is a question somewhat analogous to the notion that we should give up seeing because we are equipped with eyes.

## Hardwired

Neurotheologians have long insisted that the brain is hardwired in such a way as to predispose us to believe in God. "Rhawn Joseph, a prominent neurotheologian, goes a step further to suggest that the limbic system is dotted with 'God neurons' and 'God neurotransmitters'."[76]

Think back to Dean H. Hamer, for in his book *The God Gene*, he argues for a genetic spirituality. However, he is quick to point out that, "The first task for any scientist attempting to link genetics to spirituality is to show that spirituality can be defined and quantified."[77] For Hamer, spirituality can be viewed in the form of transcendence. In fact, "As part of a study on genetics and personality in cigarette smokers sponsored by the NCI, Hamer had previously used the Temperament and Character Inventory, which includes a self-transcendence scale developed by C. Robert Cloninger, MD, professor of psychiatry at Washington University Medical School in St. Louis. Hamer felt that Cloninger's self-transcendence scale made it possible to quantify 'people's capacity to reach out beyond themselves — to see everything in the world as part of one great totality.'"[78]

The fact is, perhaps we *do* process information in ways that bias us toward religious experience, but that does not necessarily lead to discounting either the potential use or purpose behind their existence. Indeed, one might rather conclude in order to become a nonbeliever, you must reeducate yourself. However, in fairness, we should also consider the counter argument. If spirituality is hardwired in the brain, are we to believe that agnostics and atheists have defective brains? I mean, why are their brains resistant or lacking this hardwired faculty — or are they? For it's also equally valid to ask the question, were they simply educated away from believing? Michael Shermer once told me in an interview that he changed from his evangelical ways as a product of his education. That is, he learned better. Is that really learning better? From a practical reasoning perspective and/or a purely pragmatic point of view, I think not. Why? We have already touched on some reasons, but we'll pursue this question more in the upcoming chapters.

Chapter 12

# Reasonable and Rational Conclusion

*Somewhere between the intellectual idea of why we're*
*attracted to certain things and the pragmatic reality is some*
*form of ever-evolving truth.*
~ Billy Corgan

Many people shy away from spirituality because critics, skeptics, and atheistic pundits argue that it is *irrational* to believe such things. However, if we can agree that practical reasoning (how we should act) should seek good, then we must conclude based on the evidence discussed to now, that reason dictates the reasonableness of holding to spiritual beliefs. So, it is *as rational* if not *more rational* to believe than not. If *practical reasoning* is the basis for my belief, then it is reason that supports my position. What's unreasonable about that?

However, before we move on, I have two cautions for you. First, spirituality should not be confused with the kind of dogma that clings to mutually exclusive propositions, is unscientific, and/or teaches fear and harm. Indeed, religious or spiritual practices that injure, deride, or in some other way sabotage the dignity of the human condition would not satisfy our prerequisite: good. And second, I am not saying that God necessarily exists or that there is any so-called *truth* to spiritual practices, but only that it is *rational to believe*.

## Pragmatics

Pragmatics is a term often used by the brilliant psychologist/ philosopher William James. Pragmatism is a philosophical movement that includes those who claim that an ideology or proposition is true if it works satisfactorily, that the meaning of a proposition is to be found in the practical consequences of accepting it, and that unpractical ideas are to be rejected.[79]

If the value of belief should be based on its practical consequences, then we also have to consider the many atrocities carried out in the name of religion. Many people choose to focus on the many heinous acts and therefore choose to reject religion altogether. However, as we have now seen, there are many pragmatic advantages to spiritual and religious beliefs. Consequently, those who reject spirituality deny themselves the rewards obtained from a spiritual life by using that old broad-brush standard and condemning all spirituality on the basis of the actions of some. There's nothing new about this sort of blame game, but it is worth thinking again about the many benefits you lose by making the choice not to believe.

Many of us have or will face circumstances in our lives where we feel we need some sort of redemption. We will all suffer losses of loved ones and have an urgent need to understand those losses as well as hope, believe, that there is more. There is a real pragmatic advantage in these instances inherent in a belief in a higher power.

The fact is, believing in something bigger than yourself, something that is uplifting, actually promotes health and happiness. All you need do then is to look carefully at the faith you practice and at its core teachings — are they generally altruistic? Do they encourage you, teach love and forgiveness, and fill your being with hope and joy? If the answer is yes, then the religious and spiritual practice is probably both practical and rational as well as healthy for the individual and society at large.

In the next section, we'll examine yet another valid reason to at least question the so-called finite mechanistic reductionist view found amongst agnostics and atheists alike. In my mind, and based on my personal experience, the white crows beg us to believe.

# Chapter 13

# White Crows

*If you wish to upset the law that all crows are black,*
*You mustn't seek to show that no crows are,*
*It is enough if you prove one single crow to be white.*
~ William James

Let me begin by suggesting that not all so-called white crows are naturally white. Indeed, there are hucksters who have offered us many whitewashed crows. That said, there are events many people have experienced that challenge science for an explanation. Some might be pure coincidence, but many are so stark in nature as to make the notion of coincidence a mathematical improbability plus some. But I'm getting ahead of myself.

I have spent most of my life investigating the world of comparative religion, esoteric spirituality, secular humanism, and the nature of being human. I have had a few epiphanies along the way, but they have been uniquely mine. What do I mean by that? The nature of my uncoverings and metaphysical insights are largely outgrowths of my personal experience, predisposed perhaps by the lens of some old memories. The great thing about this is that once you have a genuinely felt experience, whether it is the thrill of a particularly daring amusement park ride or the aha undergirding a transcendental moment of awe, you own it. It is yours and you know exactly how it made you feel and how you processed the event mentally. There is no ambiguity—it is with perspicuity that you proceed. The downfall is that usually your existential knowledge is relative to you and you alone. Let me flesh this out in more detail.

## Stories I shared in Mind, Meaning and Mysteries

In 2010, I wrote the book *What Does That Mean?* The purpose of this book was to show the reader how they could discover the meaning to their own lives by looking back and observing the patterns that had brought them to where they now are. In this book, I shared a number of personal stories that made a huge impact on my life path, in some instances causing me to do a 180-degree change in direction. Some of these events could be described as supernatural. *What Does That Mean?* however, was not supposed to be a book about all the white crows in my life; rather it was designed to prompt the reader to look at the unexplained events in their own lives that they have overlooked and/or relegated to the back of their mind because there was no real rational explanation. Take the next example for one.

## Train Accident

When I was a teenager, an uninsured motorist rear-ended my vehicle. The fellow's father agreed to pay me for the repairs, so one evening with my date, a beautiful young woman named Connie Bennet, I set out to pick up the money due me before going to a dance. We were driving in a 1957 Oldsmobile and on the outskirts of the small town of Woods Cross, Utah, when I began to tease Connie that we were running out of gas. It was very dark, and I stepped on the gas and then let off quickly, thereby causing the car to jerk and lunge. We were approaching several sets of railroad tracks, and as we climbed up onto one, the car engine died. As if on cue, signal arms descended, and lights began to flash. To my left I could see the headlight of the train engine bearing down on us. It seemed to be coming very fast so when Connie asked if we should get out of the car, the only thing I could think of was Connie stumbling and the car being dragged over her, so I said, "No, let me try and start the car." I turned the key, realizing the engine was flooded, and held the gas to the floor while I did so.

Connie had her hand on my leg while I frantically tried to start the engine. The next thing I knew—I was not in the car. To be absolutely clear, I was somehow in the car when the train violently collided with us and not there when Connie was being freed.

As Connie was cut from the wreckage—and this took some time—she asked about me. The driver's side of the automobile had been crushed under the cattle guard before the car was spun and dragged down the tracks. As a result, the driver's side was only three feet high or so. As it turned out, the train consisted of approximately 100 cars and was traveling at about 100 miles per hour. I know this because of the ensuing court case, for Connie was injured and wore a neck brace, and I carried around a tremendous sense of guilt.

The first thing I knew after the train hit us was that I was standing alone in a field alongside the railroad tracks, perhaps seventy-five yards or more from many emergency vehicles, all with their lights flashing. Several automobiles were backed up behind the now-stopped train. Some time had clearly elapsed because Connie was not still being extracted from the car. No, she was in an ambulance, about to leave for the hospital. My first thoughts were about her, so I ran to the emergency vehicles, where I was questioned. I was taken to Connie as soon as those in charge learned that I had been driving the car.

What I have just shared with you is not possible—but it happened. Now I fully understand how fantastic this story sounds, and I have to confess that, before I wrote about it in *What Does That Mean?* I flew into Salt Lake City so I could meet with Connie and have her verify the story. It had been many years since I had seen Connie, but her memories were the same as mine. She was sitting next to me when the train's cattle guard struck the car, dragging it down the tracks and literally crushing the driver's side of the car. In fact, and again, the car was so crushed that the passenger side required cutting in order to get Connie out of the vehicle.

There is no rational means by which this story can be explained. If it's not possible, then how do we account for it and stories like it? The accident was a physical event; two witnesses lived through it; everyone close to the event was in awe of what happened, but no one had an explanation.

As an interesting aside, I shared this story on *Coast-to-Coast AM* one evening, and the next day I heard from a listener who used reverse speech technology to examine my answer to the question asked by host George Noory, "How is that possible, Eldon?" My answer: "I have no idea." According to the listener, her examination revealed that what I was saying when reversed was, "Light is elastic." Is light elastic? Are we, as some say, light beings, vibrating at slower and therefore denser material rates? Both the question and the answer are above my pay grade, but I found the comment interesting.

Since that show I was introduced to the work of physicist Cynthia Larson. Cynthia is a graduate of Berkeley University, and she has recorded a number of instances of what she refers to as quantum jumps. She explains these jumps as tunneling in time and space. Is that far out or possible? I have no idea, but Cynthia has shared with me a number of cases that, like mine, have no reasonable scientific explanation. If you can tunnel — how did I know this was possible and why don't I remember how it was done? I tend to think that if tunneling has traction, it's something under the control of a force outside of me.

## Stories from Others

It is very interesting when you start to share extraordinary stories, as this very process seems to awaken similar memories in others. One evening while being interviewed on late-night radio about my book, *What Does That Mean? Exploring Mind, Meaning, and Mysteries*, a listener, Gene, sent me this story.

Just finished listening to your program and understand that you're collecting stories... my life has been filled with such events, though not all dramatic. To keep it brief, the one I'll share now involves my mother. At the time she was seventy-four. She had come through several different cancers and had now been diagnosed with stage four lung cancer... pretty much out of the blue. She was a rather short and hefty woman, and of late, it was getting harder for her to walk so we'd gone over to the wheelchair for any distance. We'd just come home from the last doctor's appointment, and as we reached the door of the house, she said she couldn't stand anymore. I got her inside and up a few stairs where she sat down upon the top step to rest. That was it... she couldn't get up. We were alone at the time, so it was up to me to get her moving.

What followed was more like a comedy routine as we tried to figure out how to get her up the final step, into the kitchen, and on a chair. I'm not a lightweight myself, so I had some amount of strength, but she was dead weight and every time and angle of lifting her just wasn't working. I was dragging the poor woman back and forth over the floor as we tried new ideas. Anyone I called wasn't available, so I finally asked the Angels for help. I brought in a sturdier dining room chair, placed it next to her, explained what I was going to do, that I wanted her to put her arms around my neck and I would lift. I asked for the Angels' help at this point. On the count of three I lifted... WOOSH!!... suddenly she was up and in the chair. My mother let out a gasp. I, too, was startled... it was like lifting air! I could have just been waving my hands in space. My mother asked what I did, and I had to admit nothing because it wasn't me that lifted her that time.

In the time that followed prior to her death, there was one experience after another... the angelic realm was my hospice team. Even a friend who had come to visit remarked that the house felt full, like there were many people around and wanted to know who it was that she heard walking. My dog was always reacting to various things as well.

How does one verify this information? For Gene, verification is obvious as a result of the experience! It may be subjective, but so are most of our lives. The fact is, we know our lives only as a result of subjective experience. Everything about us is essentially wired in a loop, as Douglas Hofstadter explains in his book, *I Am a Strange Loop*. Our self-awareness is a self-reference, and this is entirely subjective. I may only introduce the objective when it is outside of inner self. That is to say, the way we know ourselves is through consciousness, not primarily a mirror. Our bodies change over time and sometimes so drastically that if we failed to have a regular reference to the changes, we may well fail to recognize ourselves. It is our consciousness through which we know ourselves, and our experiences or interpretations thereof. This means we live our lives primarily in the subjective realm.

One of the problems with many stories of the sort Gene shares exists in the inability to replicate and thereby verify the experience independently. It can be easy for wishful thinking to interpret events along the lines of our predisposition, and so many cynics dismiss accounts like Gene's, not as evidence of a white crow but rather as their personal anecdotal interpretation. Think about that.

I have had the pleasure to meet and chat with many people from all walks of life, all socioeconomic status, and it is very rare for someone to inform me that they have never had some strange event in their lives that defied standard reasonable explanation.

Another story, perhaps more dramatic, was sent in by Evelyn.

Many years ago, when my (now) husband and I were dating, we were taking one of our customary Saturday evening walks in Brooklyn, New York along Flatbush Avenue. We were lost in the moment, chatting animatedly, not paying much attention to where we were when we heard a loud explosion from behind where we had just been. A restaurant storefront was on fire; the stove had exploded sending shards of glass into the street where we had walked only seconds before. We looked at each other, confused and dazed, both thinking, "It was only one minute!"

What do you think? Was this one just coincidence? The secular humanist would have a full explanation for an event of this nature, and it would not necessitate calling upon anything supernatural. Still, does that invalidate the experience for the person experiencing it?

There are very many miraculous stories if you take time to listen. Some stretch our imagination, and many are purely subjective, but there are also those where objective evidence exists. For example, in my own train wreck, there were witnesses, court transcripts, and so forth. That said, the fact is, as explained in the journal article appearing in *Sociology of Religion* published by Oxford University Press, "Miracles are positively correlated with life satisfaction and partially protect against the negative effects of stress on life satisfaction."[80] They are not uncommon, and they have a profound influence on our lives.

I would encourage all of you to think back through your life for the large and small miracles. It might be the time you prayed for some extra money and the next day found a fresh $100 bill in your jacket. It might be the voice that warned you against doing something, and it turned out to be very wise guidance. It might be the time you put a cross on your dog to heal her, and it worked. It might be something as simple as knowing who was on the phone before you answered it, or knowing something dreadful had just happened before you learned about it. All of these examples are from stories that have been shared with me, and there are many more. The point is: *We all have them!*

## So, What Do They All Mean?

All right, each of these stories have a common denominator but not an objective method by which we can say with a certainty that a supernatural force was involved. We certainly cannot replicate the events so the notion of conducting some scientific study is out of the question, but that doesn't by itself invalidate anything. For example, we all know about Napoleon, but should we decide to replicate his experience at Waterloo, no search for talent, that is, finding a short person who places his hand in his vest and rides a white horse, and/or in finding the men to replicate the facing armies, would satisfactorily duplicate the event. Understanding this leads to some clarity when it comes to both historical reports as well as your personal experiences! And in that sense, events of this nature are both valuable and yet outside of the realm of scientific verification.

Now before striking again at my point, here's one more story to digest that I shared in my book, *I Believe: When What You Believe Matters*:

A small child ran to a home overlooking a cliff and pounded on the door in the middle of the night. When the owner opened the door, the child called for help and led the person to the cliff's edge, where the automobile he'd been riding in with his mother, father, and siblings could be seen. It was crushed and broken apart, and his family members were all dead. The car had been traveling too fast to negotiate a hard turn during a heavy rainstorm and had sailed off the cliff. When law enforcement officers asked the child how he got out of the vehicle, he answered, "A giant hand reached into the car, lifted me out, and set me on the side of the road."[81]

There is another story that is becoming a legend of sorts — so much so that even *Snopes* has verified it. It is the story of a choir who missed a fire. *Snopes* reports the story this way:

As unbelievable as the story may seem, it did happen—even though a Nebraska church exploded one evening in 1950 just five minutes after choir practice had been scheduled to begin, not one of the fifteen people who should have been present was injured because none had yet arrived when the building collapsed: Choir practice at the West Side Baptist Church in Beatrice, Nebraska, always began at 7:20 on Wednesday evening. At 7:25 p.m. on Wednesday, March 1, 1950, an explosion demolished the church. The blast forced a nearby radio station off the air and shattered windows in surrounding homes. But every one of the choir's fifteen members escaped injury, saved by a fortuitous coincidence: All were late for practice that night. Considering the sanctified site of the explosion, it was not surprising that some attributed the near miss to divine intervention.

They supposed rightly that the odds of unanimous tardiness were slim indeed, especially when the reasons were examined. Car trouble delayed two women. The minister and his wife and daughter were delayed by a dress that needed ironing at the last minute. Others were late because they paused to complete homework, finish a letter, or hear the end of a favorite radio show. One awoke late from a nap. Some could think of no special reason; they were just late.

It is impossible to calculate precise odds for all these events occurring at once. But past performance indicated that each person would be late for practice one time in four— producing a one-in-a-million chance that the entire choir would be late that night.[82]

Stories of this nature abound, as do the many unexplained and inexplicable little things that every human being experiences at some point in their lives. All of these stories among the hundreds of millions of people who have at one time or another experienced an otherwise unexplainable event, would in aggregate overwhelm our ability to argue with them. In other words, there is power in numbers. I'm not saying that all of the stories are indeed miracles, but I am arguing that there are very many white crows. Again, as William James put it, you need not prove that all crows are black—you need only one white crow to disprove it.

The question then becomes, when is a white crow truly a white crow and how are we to know? This, too, lends itself to subjective interpretation, for is one in a million sufficient odds to say the choir didn't survive due to coincidence, but rather to some other unseen influence?

## Consciousness at a Distance

Most of us have experienced a situation where we seemed to think the same thing and/or know what our closest friends were thinking. Maybe we said the same thing at the same time, or had the same response only to look at each other and smile. Are minds communicating when this happens? Mind to mind— consciousness at a distance?

According to the research, the answer is yes. Take this study for example:

A brain-to-brain communication study organized by Harvard Medical School has revealed that human brains can "talk" directly to one another despite being physically separated by thousands of miles. Conducted by a group of robotics engineers and neuroscientists from across the globe, the study proves that information can be transmitted between two human brains through leveraging different passageways to the mind.

Conducted by the Director of the Berenson-Allen Center for Noninvasive Brain Stimulation at Beth Israel Deaconess Medical Center (BIDMC) and a Professor of Neurology at Harvard Medical School, the researchers initiated a computer-meditated brain-to-brain transmission from a city in India to a city in France.[83]

In an article appearing in *Science News* under the title, "How You and Your Friends Can Play a Video Game Together Using Only Your Minds," researchers created a method for two people to help a third person solve a task using only their minds.

Telepathic communication might be one step closer to reality thanks to new research from the University of Washington. A team created a method that allows three people to work together to solve a problem using only their minds. In BrainNet, three people play a Tetris-like game using a brain-to-brain interface. This is the first demonstration of two things: a brain-to-brain network of more than two people, and a person being able to both receive and send information to others using only their brain... "Humans are social beings who communicate with each other to cooperate and solve problems that none of us can solve on our own," said corresponding author Rajesh Rao, the CJ and Elizabeth Hwang professor in the UW's Paul G. Allen School of Computer Science & Engineering and a co-director of the Center for Neurotechnology. "We wanted to know if a group of people could collaborate using only their brains. That's how we came up with the idea of BrainNet: where two people help a third person solve a task."[84]

There are a number of new studies appearing now that tend to support the idea that minds do indeed have the ability to communicate across distance. Although still somewhat controversial amidst the scientific community, this quote from *F1000 Research*, titled *Brain-to-Brain (Mind-To-Mind) Interaction at Distance: A Confirmatory Study*, sums up the general position taken today:

... The examination of potential statistical artifacts revealed a good level of coincidences in only four pairs using a new procedure to detect the sequences of silence and signal between the EEG activity of the pairs of participants, giving a mild support to the hypothesis that two brains and hence two minds can be connected at distance.[85]

If minds communicate at a distance, does this offer any more evidence favoring spirituality? Many have argued that it does. For example, Dr. Dean Radin, lead scientist for the Institute of Noetic Sciences, is convinced that much of what is generally attached to spiritual thinking, especially within the New Age groups, such as telepathy, precognition, psychokinesis, and clairvoyance, can be demonstrated scientifically as valid. If so, does this gives rise somehow automatically to the inference that the spiritual domain is real? Does mind acting on random number generators, evidence of clairvoyance, etc., imply spirituality? I don't think so. It certainly implies that mind is not the local event that many agnostics and atheists have posited, but perhaps we'll come to understand one day the mechanic behind these phenomena, if indeed Radin's argument turns out to be true.

In a conversation with Dr. Radin discussing his book, *Real Magic: Ancient Wisdom, Modern Science, and a Guide to the Secret Power of the Universe*, he referred to a number of studies that I admit swayed me. However, since the mind appears to work only with a brain, and the brain is an electromagnetic "machine," it is reasonable to expect that one day we'll understand more specifically how "mind at a distance" may work. After all, radio waves and brain waves are both forms of electromagnetic radiation. The brain emits waves all of the time and especially at times when a person focuses attention or remembers something of significance.

I'm personally of the opinion that we will unmask the mechanism that explains the matter of "mind at a distance" and it won't continue to hold the implied connection to the spiritual that many give it today. The proverbial flashlight to a Neanderthal may have implied godhead, but it certainly fails to actually represent any such thing. Indeed, I hesitated to include this discussion in the book because I find it to be a bit of a red herring. I do not believe that everything we fail to be able to explain necessarily therefore implies a higher power. That said, since the idea of "mind at a distance" can be so immersed in the spiritual beliefs of some, I thought it derelict to avoid the issue. Much like illustrating in earlier chapters the inconsistencies inherent in many religious definitions, I deemed it appropriate to put this argument under some scrutiny as part of my own fairness doctrine. That said, there remain some other considerations not yet attended to.

## Stories from the Dead

There are some stories that are difficult, if not impossible, to explain that are allegedly the result of communication with the deceased. Not long ago I spoke with Michael Tymn about several of the cases discussed in his book, *The Articulate Dead*. Tymn is a meticulous researcher who is more than willing to call a fraud a fraud. However, again in fairness, he sees no reason to answer the skeptics and is probably more inclined to accept some things than I would. That said, let's take this striking case shared by Tymn as an example of communication with the dead. The John D. Fox family moved into a small home in Hydesville, New York. Quoting Tymn:

> Shortly after moving into the house on December 11, 1847, the family of four, including two daughters, Margaret, fourteen, and Kate, eight, began hearing strange raps and taps, but it wasn't until March 31 [1848] that the two daughters realized that they could communicate with the raps by snapping their fingers. Upon learning of this, Mrs. Fox asked the "raps"

to respond to questions by giving two raps for "yes" and silence for "no." She asked if a human being was making the raps. There was no response. When she asked, "Is it a spirit?" there were two raps. Neighbors were called in and dozens of questions were put to the "spirit." It was determined that the communicating spirit had been murdered in the house about five years earlier, before the Fox family moved in.

The questioning of this nature went on for days, and it was further determined that the communicating spirit's body had been buried beneath the house. Digging began, and at the depth of five feet, human hair and bones were found.[86]

Now again in fairness, the Fox sisters were or became mediums as a result of this case, but after P.T. Barnum convinced them to join his sideshow, their credibility was compromised. I have no intention of discussing some of the many other cases witnessed by very credible people involving the Fox sisters before their Barnum casting, for that is not the purview of this book. This one case is well documented, and I'll let it stand on its own. After all, it would appear to be a white crow in my opinion.

There are many other cases of afterlife communication through living channels that could be brought to bear at this time. However, one white crow is all we need, and my purpose here does not include saturating the argument that belief in an afterlife is *not* irrational with talk of mediums and channels.

## Reincarnation

Okay, let's look at reincarnation, for if there is any such thing, then the strength in the proposition that there is an afterlife, and therefore a high probability of a higher power, grows exponentially. Of course, there are disproven cases such as the now infamous Bridey Murphy matter.[87] That said, there are many cases that challenge even the most skeptical for an explanation.

In an article titled "The Evidence for Reincarnation," Ervin Laszlo and Anthony Peake tell us this:

The pioneering research on recent reincarnation stories is the work of Ian Stevenson, a Canadian-American psychiatrist who worked at the University of Virginia School of Medicine. During more than four decades, Stevenson investigated the reincarnation-type experiences of thousands of children, both in the West and in the East. Some of the past-life memories recounted by the children have been verified as the experience of a person who had lived previously and whose death matched the impressions reported by the child. Sometimes the child carried a birthmark associated with the death of the person with whom he or she identified, such as an indentation or discoloration on the part of the body where a fatal bullet entered, or a malformation on a hand or the foot the deceased had lost.

In a path-breaking essay published in 1958, "The Evidence for Survival from Claimed Memories of Former Incarnations," Stevenson analyzed the evidence from reincarnation stories of children and presented narratives on seven of the cases. These past-life cases turned out to be verifiable, with the incidents recounted by the children recorded in often obscure local journals and articles.[88]

Their article shares five stories that strongly argue for reincarnation. I have chosen only one to present here, for we need only one white crow.

[A] typical Stevenson case was that of Swarnlata Mishra, born in a small village in Madhya Pradesh in 1948. When she was three years old, she began having spontaneous past-life memories of being a girl called Biya Pathak, who lived in a village more than 100 miles away. She described that the house Biya lived in had four rooms and was painted white.

She began to sing songs that she claimed she used to know, together with complex dance routines that were unknown to her present family and friends. Six years later she recognized some people who had been her friends in the past life. This stimulated her father to start writing down what she said and searching for proof of her reincarnation.

Her case generated interest outside of the village. One investigator who visited the city discovered that a woman who matched the description given by Swarnlata had died nine years previously. Investigations subsequently confirmed that a young girl called Biya had lived in just such a house in that town.

Swarnlata's father decided to take his daughter to the town and to have her introduced to members of Biya's family. As a test to see if she indeed was a reincarnated personality, the family introduced people who were not related to the child. Swarnlata immediately identified these individuals as being imposters. Indeed, some details of her past life memories were so precise that all were amazed.[89]

Are these genuine white crows? — you must decide. However, if you're interested, your local library no doubt is full of volumes of information on reincarnation and afterlife communication — but I would caution you to not believe everything you read.

# Part Three: Synthesis

## Choosing a Belief

*Believe that life is worth living and your belief will help create the fact.*
~ William James

We all have beliefs — spiritual beliefs, life beliefs, political beliefs, and so forth. It is fair to cross-examine those beliefs from time to time, interrogating them for both their integrity and how they serve or direct our lives. Think about how your beliefs guide your thoughts and actions and ask the big question, "Does this belief give rise to promoting my highest best in health and happiness? Does it make me a better person?"

If your beliefs fail to improve the quality of your life, you may want to rethink them. In this section we'll consider how it is that we come to some of our knowledge and conclusions.

# Chapter 14

# Noetics and Paragnosis

*There is a beauty and clarity that comes from simplicity that we sometimes do not appreciate in our thirst for intricate solutions.*
~ Dieter F. Uchtdorf

Paragnosis is defined as knowledge that cannot be obtained by normal means—knowledge which can only be gained through extraordinary or supernatural means. Where there are many who have argued the Blank Slate theory (Tabula Rosa), it is a given that we do not come into the world a blank slate. John Locke most famously insisted that individuals are born without built-in mental content and that therefore all knowledge comes from experience or perception. Innatism by contrast argues that the mind comes into the world with certain knowledge. For example, no one needs to teach us that there is no such number so large that we cannot add one to it.

Noetics is a branch of metaphysics dealing with the study of mind. Noetic discussions, such as those by Aristotle in *Metaphysics*, sought to explain how the human intellect goes from its original condition (the natural state), a state without thought, to the human state (the active state) where it thinks. The One Intellect, what Aristotle refers to as the Unmoved Mover, is equated with the active intellect of all. In this sense, our very active individual intellect is connected directly to the One active intellect. One might argue that implicit in this proposition is the notion that the formative fetus exists in a state without thought until developed enough to think. It is interesting that ensoulment for Aristotle, and therefore the active state where thinking occurs, differed according to the sex. "In the time of Aristotle, it was widely believed that the human soul entered the forming body at forty days (male embryos) or ninety days (female embryos), and quickening was an indication of the presence of a soul."[90]

When you consider this proposition of One active intellect, shared and available to all, for a moment—it is easy to understand why so many have concluded that inspiration, creativity, the arts, sciences, and so much are really the thoughts (or energy) of God. Is it possible to open up and receive transmissions directly from the Unmoved Mover? Is it also possible to ignore these transmissions completely and get on with our own private agendas? And is it therefore also possible to construe something as a transmission that absolutely is no such thing?

Noetics is often used to explain how we know something we have no knowledge of ever learning. Daniel Kahneman refers to this as "rapid cognition." Kahneman authored the idea of system 1 and system 2 thinking—fast and slow. Fleshed out with respect to rapid cognition, we have this:

> Intuition is the result of the associative thinking that takes place in the unconscious (System 1). The unconscious sees patterns and connects dots our conscious brain (System 2) isn't even aware of. It operates quickly and it's always on. That's because, by the way, it's what keeps us alive. And keeping us alive is what our brain is designed to do. System 1 makes rapid-fire assessments and communicates them to System 2. When we become consciously aware of one of those assessments, we call it intuition. We could also call it jumping to conclusions.[91]

John Bargh refers to it as "automatic processing."[92] Bargh is particularly famous for his demonstrations of priming affecting action. In my conversation with Professor Bargh, we discussed this priming effect. A priming effect occurs whenever the exposure to one thing is paired with another and can affect thinking and/or alter behavior. For example, a child is shown their favorite candy sitting on a park bench. The next time they see a park bench, they think of their candy and in some instances may even salivate over the taste of their candy.

Bargh has carried out a number of studies using words to prime subjects. One of his most quoted studies presented words relating to elderliness. The reported result found that subjects primed with ageing words walk slower when exiting the lab than subjects not so primed.[93] Where there is some controversy about this particular study, there is little or none regarding the influence of words to prime action. Priming effects are well studied, and the bottom line is this: we are influenced, including by subliminal stimuli, despite the absence of any conscious awareness.[94]

So, the question arises: Is knowing without how we know really only automatic processing or rapid cognition? These explanations may well work with what we call intuition, but do they really work with other forms of knowing?

Most commonly think of this sort of intuition as a gut feeling, an instinct, a hunch, an inner voice, and so forth. Some things fit this category, but others deny the idea that somehow rapid or automatic thinking was somehow engaged. For example, we may have a sort of premonition about a friend we suddenly have an urge to speak to. The phone rings and our friend is on the other end. Is this intuition? If so, then neither automatic processing nor rapid cognition explains this phenomenon. Most of us have experienced something like this and there are many reports of people knowing of an accident involving a loved one that occurred miles away.

There is another form of knowing without knowing how you know that doesn't fit with our understanding of intuition/ rapid cognition. How, for example, can someone suddenly gain mathematic genius due to a blow on the head? I spoke with Jason Padgett of Seattle, Washington about exactly this phenomenon.

Jason is an example of acquired savant syndrome. Jason was not a math genius before being mugged one night leaving a bar where he'd had a few. However, when he came to in the hospital, he was instantly a number theorist and now views the attack and its effects as a gift, despite the fact that the attack also left him with OCD and PTSD.[95]

There is also the notion of claircognizance. Those who propose this idea define it this way, "It is where your guides, or perhaps even your higher self, simply makes direct contact with your mind."[96] This form of cognition is thought of as psychic awareness, and I will leave it at that for the moment since our discussion at this point is as much about definitions as anything else in our attempt to comprehend what knowing without knowing how we know might be.

One thing is certain; knowing without knowing how we know is not uncommon. For myself, this question was resolved for me very early in life. When I was in high school, I walked into a geometry class, opened the book, and somehow knew everything in it. How was that possible? How could I know the theorems of geometry without ever studying it? As an aside, I decided to fool around in the class, so I'd lay my head down and pretend to sleep. This provoked the teacher on many occasions, and he would call on me with some abstract question from our text. I would smile and flippantly respond—always with the correct answer. I suppose this is what children do, or at least some children. I remember being pleased that I somehow knew everything, but did I really examine how this was possible? Not until many years later.

There are many possible explanations. Some might say it's a past life memory. Others might argue that perhaps I had been exposed to it when I was very young and failed to remember this context. Still others would explain it on the basis of the collective unconscious[97] or tapping into the One Mind. One might get truly creative and compare the acquisition of this knowledge with acquired savant syndrome. For example, as I mentioned earlier, Jason Padgett told me of how he was mugged one evening, and when he awoke, he saw the world in perfect fractals. I had the opportunity to interview Dr. Darold A. Treffert, author of *Islands of Genius*. Treffert has made it a career to investigate autism and savant syndrome. In his opinion, if we consider the savants' lives, we can more fully and properly understand the gifts they live with. Whatever the answer, you must decide the explanation you choose, but the fact remains, I knew geometry without knowing how I knew.

The entire issue encompassed by acquired savant syndrome begs many questions. From where does this genius arise? Do we all have latent knowledge that goes untapped until and unless some sudden blow or something allows the brain to access it? How is that possible? Is there one mind and somehow we suddenly tap into it but only get a fraction of what might be there? I mean, for one it is mathematical genius, for another it may be musical genius — it seems never to be "all" genius. In other words, only some portion, some specialty, seems to be gained with our acquired savants.

Knowing something and not knowing how we know is not a totally unusual experience. Many people, probably including you the reader, have experienced knowing something and not knowing how you knew. Was it a premonition, a dream recall, a sort of déjà vu, or something else? Who knows—but not knowing from where or why the information came to you does not change the fact that somehow you knew.

Literally all spiritual systems allow for the direct transmission of knowledge from a plane outside that of our earthly world. Does this suggest another white crow?

## Knowing Without Knowing: Is It Intuition?
Einstein stated, "The only real valuable thing is intuition." Intuition has been defined this way: "Intuition is considered

as the highest form of human intelligence. It's that unique ability to directly understand something even without logic or analytic reasoning. Although defining it is a bit of a challenge, you should pay close attention to your intuition. Most of the time, it's telling you something really important." If we are to accept this definition, then intuition itself may go beyond rapid cognition or automatic processing. Consider, for example, some of these instances.

I once asked Norman Shealy, MD, about his work and creativity. Shealy is an author and inventor with more than a dozen books and patents to his name. In a moment of self-disclosure, he confessed that his every invention had been given him… by his Guides—an inner voice that informs him of what and how to accomplish his aim. Is this intuition, rapid cognition, automatic processing, or…

Think about these examples offered by Oprah in her magazine:

**44 B.C.E.**
Calpurnia, wife of Julius Caesar, foresees her husband's assassination and begs him not to go to the senate. Caesar doesn't listen. Several stab wounds and a few famous last words later, he is dead.
**1865**
When Ulysses S. Grant is invited to join Abraham Lincoln at Ford's Theatre, Grant's wife Julia urges him not to go ("I do not know what possessed me to take such a freak," she later writes). Unlike Caesar, Grant heeds his wife's advice. It soon emerges that he, too, may have been an assassination target that night.
**1940**
Winston Churchill is dining at 10 Downing Street when a German bomb hits nearby. He orders his staff to leave the kitchen. Moments later another bomb falls, obliterating—

you guessed it—the kitchen.

**1965**

Paul McCartney hears a tune in a dream—"the most magic thing!"—but it's so unlike anything he's written, he worries he's recalling someone else's song. McCartney plays it for anyone who will listen, but no one can identify it. So, the Beatles record the track and title it "Yesterday."[98]

Many of the creative geniuses have signaled the value of intuition in their lives and writing. Alexis Carrel, a French surgeon and biologist who was awarded the Nobel Prize in Physiology or Medicine in 1912 for pioneering vascular suturing techniques, once stated, "Intuition comes very close to clairvoyance; it appears to be the extrasensory perception of reality." Albert Einstein put it this way: "I believe in intuitions and inspirations... I sometimes feel that I am right. I do not know that I am." Madeleine L'Engle, author of *A Wrinkle in Time*, had this to say: "Don't try to comprehend with your mind. Your minds are very limited. Use your intuition." Bill Gates has added, "Often you have to rely on intuition." Henri Poincaré, a French mathematician, theoretical physicist, engineer, and philosopher of science, had these words: "It is through science that we prove, but through intuition that we discover." And Dean Koontz, international bestselling author of suspense novels, used these words: "Intuition is seeing with the soul."[99]

What would you say intuition is and why? Have you ever known something and not known how you knew it? Do you have a neat tidy explanation that does not call upon an alternative model to the mechanistic reductionism of so many atheists and agnostics?

The fact is, we have all experienced this kind of knowing at some time in our lives. For most people, noetic knowing would include incidences like knowing who was on the phone before we answered it. Indeed, our animal friends may possess somewhat of this gift as well. I spoke with Dr. Rupert Sheldrake on a couple of occasions. In his book, *Dogs That Know When Their Owners Are Coming Home*, Sheldrake fleshes out a theory based on telepathy between pets and their humans. He provides a great deal of scientific findings and documents a number of cases that beg for an alternative explanation. Sheldrake can be controversial, but mainly because he is a hard scientist willing to take on science. In his book, *Science Set Free*, he clearly shows how science is constricted by its assumptions—assumptions that have hardened into dogma. He made it very clear to me in his opinion that the attack on spirituality is a protectionistic effort to reinforce a dogma of science.

## Looking for Connections

We occupy a place in history that is unique, at least from the perspective of our local awareness. We enjoy a time where information abounds, sometimes overstimulating, but always available. Unfortunately, not all of the information available is true in any real sense, and much of it actually is mis- or dis-information. Indeed, sometimes our experts tell us things they believe to be true, based on science, only to later learn just how false or foolish their claims turned out to be. We must be careful about what we believe and why, and guard against accepting only that which we want to believe.

Our very nature seeks patterns and causal connections. We somehow sense that we gain some control of matters if we but understand how and why they occur. As a result, we can draw conclusions based on connections that are unreal in any causal way. Take, for example, the notion of apophenia. Apophenia is defined as "the tendency to perceive a connection or meaningful pattern between unrelated or random things" or the idea that there is no such thing as coincidence. One who experiences extreme apophenia finds patterns in everything. They refuse to admit that coincidence, chance, and the like exist. Ergo the assumption that there are patterns and they have meaning. According to this perspective, there is nothing that occurs as a matter of chance—no such thing as accidents. If you fall, you were supposed to fall; if you dream, the dream has meaning to you, and so forth. Everything allegedly fits to a larger, more meaningful pattern.

That said, is it possible that some instances are instantiated by purpose—purpose that reveals itself by way of patterns? Are we finding a pattern where no real pattern exists? Quoting from *You Are Not So Smart*, by David McRaney:

... Apophenia is an umbrella term that encompasses other phenomena like the Texas Sharpshooter Fallacy and pareidolia. When you commit the Texas Sharpshooter Fallacy, you draw a circle around a series of random events and decide there is some meaning in the chaos that isn't really there. In pareidolia, you see shapes like clouds or tree limbs as people or faces. Apophenia is refusing to believe in clutter and noise, in coincidence and chance.[100]

## Littlewood's Law?

So now, according to scholarship, apophenia occurs most often when you feel that events in your life appear to be synchronistic. Question: do we force our interpretations of the world through a lens of convenience, one built more on emotion than reason? Take this example and I'll ask the question again. My wife has a cat, Freja, that she is very attached to. One day Freja, an indoor cat, got out of the house and went missing. Everyone searched for her—no Freja. My wife was truly upset and afraid the coyotes in and around our little ranch got her. Early one morning my wife went out again in search of Freja. No cat to be found. I mentally asked where Freja was. A picture of the cat on our property appeared in my mind. I proceeded directly there, picked up one scared dirty cat, and brought it into the house where she has remained ever since. Is this me pattern matching? Is this an example of Littlewood's Law or is there more going on here? So, again, the question: do we force our interpretations on the world? Is it true that almost everything is possible without some supernatural explanation—the so-called one-in-a-million shot, which by the way, is Littlewood's Law. Professor Littlewood made a few calculations leading to this observation: the average human being sleeps eight hours a day and some event occurs about every second in their waking lives. That means that about one million chances occur every month, so the one-in-a-million chances theme translates this way: we should expect mathematically to experience phenomenon about once a month—not such a long shot after all.

## Magical or Mechanical

All right, at some point in all of our lives, we will make a choice between a sometimes "magical" universe and a purely mechanical one. In a magical world, synchronicity can exist along with a host of other phenomena like precognitive dreams, premonitions, the spirit world, and so forth. In a strictly mechanical world, there is no such thing as life after death; near-death experiences are but REM activity (rapid eye movement associated with dreams); spiritual visions and experiences are but hallucinations of some sort, etc.—you get the point.

From my perspective, our universe is both mechanical and magical! Sometimes the mechanical aspect of our being gives rise to cause-and-effect probabilities, but sometimes other forces enter into the equation to perhaps mitigate some dreadful outcome mechanically set in motion. Take, for example, the story of the choir who escaped the fire. Do you honestly think that the choir was saved as a matter of Littlewood's Law?

Although many argue against miracles, it bears repeating: our best scientists have been wrong. Nobel prizes have been awarded for great discoveries and achievements, but not all have turned out to be so fantastic after all. Take, for example, the 1949 Nobel Prize in medicine that went to Dr. António Egas Moniz. Dr. Moniz innovated a treatment heralded by the community of medicine as the cure for many forms of mental illness. He traveled and lectured throughout the world teaching his technique and was largely embraced as nothing short of a genius. Moniz's treatment began by using an ice pick and a hammer to perform a lobotomy. The procedure was so widespread and acceptable that even President John F. Kennedy's sister, Rose Marie (Rosemary) Kennedy, underwent a prefrontal lobotomy at the age of twenty-three.

For four decades Moniz performed his $25 lobotomies—by some estimates, around 3,500 lobotomies in all. Despite his 1949 Nobel Prize, when a greater understanding of the brain finally informed all of exactly what a lobotomy was doing, Moniz fell into disrepute. His fellows turned on him like hungry dingo dogs on a wounded mate.

Over and over the public has blindly followed some puppeteer. In the past, the politician, the prophet, the scientist, the expert, and so on, have garnered both the attention and affection of the public only to disappoint them. Idols do all have their clay feet.

The point of this iteration is to offer the choice once again to you. Is the world magical, mechanical, or both?

## Decision Stories

Here are some of the stories from my own life that have caused me to decide that there is more to life than shoes and ships and sealing wax. I have written about much of this in my book, *What Does That Mean?* As I traveled around and spoke about this book, asking everyone to think about the so-called unexplained events they may have had in their lives, I was not surprised to find that literally everyone seemed to be able to recall at least one. Indeed, one of the world's most prominent agnostics,

Michael Shermer, shared an event with me during one of our conversations that is just this sort of thing. So, before I share his story with you, pause for a moment and think back on your own life. How many events can you think of that are inconsistent with some normal, ordinary explanation? Then ask yourself, why do you forget them? That seems to be another interesting aspect to consider, for many people I have spoken to not only forget them initially, but even after they recall and write them down, they somehow slip from memory again. Why?

Okay, Shermer's story in his own words as they appeared in the "Skeptic" column for *Scientific American* under the title: *I just witnessed an event so mysterious that it shook my skepticism.*

Often, I am asked if I have ever encountered something that I could not explain. What my interlocutors have in mind are not bewildering enigmas such as consciousness or U.S. foreign policy but anomalous and mystifying events that suggest the existence of the paranormal or supernatural. My answer is: yes, now I have.

The event took place on June 25, 2014. On that day I married Jennifer Graf, from Köln, Germany. She had been raised by her mom; her grandfather, Walter, was the closest father figure she had growing up, but he died when she was 16. In shipping her belongings to my home before the wedding, most of the boxes were damaged and several precious heirlooms lost, including her grandfather's binoculars. His 1978 Philips 070 transistor radio arrived safely, so I set out to bring it back to life after decades of muteness. I put in new batteries and opened it up to see if there were any loose connections to solder. I even tried "percussive maintenance," said to work on such devices — smacking it sharply against a hard surface. Silence. We gave up and put it at the back of a desk drawer in our bedroom.

Three months later, after affixing the necessary signatures to our marriage license at the Beverly Hills courthouse, we returned home, and in the presence of my family said our vows and exchanged rings. Being 9,000 kilometers from family, friends and home, Jennifer was feeling amiss and lonely. She wished her grandfather were there to give her away. She whispered that she wanted to say something to me alone, so we excused ourselves to the back of the house where we could hear music playing in the bedroom. We don't have a music system there, so we searched for laptops and iPhones and even opened the back door to check if the neighbors were playing music. We followed the sound to the printer on the desk, wondering—absurdly—if this combined printer/scanner/fax machine also included a radio. Nope.

At that moment Jennifer shot me a look I haven't seen since the supernatural thriller, *The Exorcist*, startled audiences. "That can't be what I think it is, can it?" she said. She opened the desk drawer and pulled out her grandfather's transistor radio, out of which a romantic love song wafted. We sat in stunned silence for minutes. "My grandfather is here with us," Jennifer said, tearfully. "I'm not alone."

Shortly thereafter we returned to our guests with the radio playing as I recounted the backstory. My daughter, Devin, who came out of her bedroom just before the ceremony began, added, "I heard the music coming from your room just as you were about to start." The odd thing is that we were there getting ready just minutes before that time, sans music.

Later that night we fell asleep to the sound of classical music emanating from Walter's radio. Fittingly, it stopped working the next day and has remained silent ever since. What does this mean? Had it happened to someone else I might suggest a chance electrical anomaly and the law of large numbers as an explanation—with billions of people having billions of experiences every day, there's bound to be a handful of extremely unlikely events that stand out in their timing and meaning. In any case, such anecdotes do not constitute scientific evidence that the dead survive or that they can communicate with us via electronic equipment.

Jennifer is as skeptical as I am when it comes to paranormal and supernatural phenomena. Yet the eerie conjunction of these deeply evocative events gave her the distinct feeling that her grandfather was there and that the music was his gift of approval. I have to admit, it rocked me back on my heels and shook my skepticism to its core as well. I savored the experience more than the explanation.

The emotional interpretations of such anomalous events grant them significance regardless of their causal account. And if we are to take seriously the scientific credo to keep an open mind and remain agnostic when the evidence is indecisive or the riddle unsolved, we should not shut the doors of perception when they may be opened to us to marvel in the mysterious.[101]

We all experience anomalous events, and we interpret them according to our own bias. Any event may or may not mean anything more than you assign it. On the other hand, confirmation bias works just as well with the agnostic/atheist as it does with the believer.

So, here's another story of my own. My wife Ravinder decided she wanted a home birth with our first son. This frightened me, I must admit. She was rather insistent and assured me that midwifery was sophisticated enough that there was nothing to worry about. At the time we lived in Big Bear, California. Any real emergencies required a trip down the mountain for proper care. Now my wife had a dear friend who was also pregnant and planning on doing a home birth as well. I had little chance of persuading Ravinder differently.

One evening in late November, Ravinder's water broke. The midwives were called. The next day the midwife came up the mountain and Ravinder's pregnant friend arrived at the house. They walked her, coached her, and worked with her for the entire day and into the night. Somewhere around 11 p.m. they crashed wherever they could find to stretch out. I was in my home office when it was made very clear to me that the baby needed to come now and would if I got Ravinder up. There was a true sense of urgency to this notification that I can only describe as a silent verbal instruction.

I went to our bedroom and told Ravinder it was time and she had to get up. She was thoroughly exhausted and resisted at first, but trusting me, she got out of bed. I took her to the sitting room where she could stand and hold my shoulders. Her uterus was tipped so I angled how she stood. I had no experience with this sort of thing so to this day I'm not certain how I knew what she had to do, but I followed my instructions. I assured her that the baby would come in ten to fifteen minutes. Unbeknownst to me, the midwife had called her supervisor because of her concern. However, when I got Ravinder up, the midwife was very upset with me, insisting Ravinder needed to rest, and I didn't know what I was doing. She even tried to tell me that I was standing Ravinder wrong because of her tipped uterus.

I informed the midwife that Ravinder would give birth in the next ten to fifteen minutes so bugger off (LOL). I don't exactly remember what I did tell her, and it probably was not that nice. Just as the midwife began to scold me again, her boss arrived. She knelt down under my wife while the midwife explained how terrible this action of mine was and how ridiculous the idea that the baby would arrive in the next ten minutes. Her boss, seeing the baby crown, looked up at the midwife and told her, "He's right."

Our eldest son was born exactly as I had said. I am convinced to this day that had I not acted on the inner voice, the birth of our son would have had undesirable consequences. Intuition? I think more, much more than intuition was at work here. What do you think?

Here's another one for you. When I was in kindergarten, I shot marbles in the playground at lunch. I wasn't a bad marble shooter (probably pretty cocky about it at the time) so one afternoon I won a couple handfuls of marbles. We shot marbles to keep, so the winner kept the marbles they had shot out of the ring (a circle drawn in the dirt). When the bell rang, I gathered up my marbles and ran back to class.

Inside the classroom I reviewed my win, including a couple of lovely tiger-eye marbles. It was then I discovered my taw missing. My taw was my shooting marble, and there was no other marble that fit my fingers like my taw. Not too slick, not too sticky, not too big, not too small—just perfect. I nearly panicked. I wanted to jump up and run outside that very minute.

When school ended, I went out to find my taw. I searched and searched and came up empty. By the time I became so upset that I was nearly frantic, everyone had left, and I was alone on the school grounds. I stopped, probably ready to cry, when an inner voice told me to close my eyes. I did as instructed. I was then told to take a certain number of steps (like ten or twelve—I don't remember exactly) straight ahead. I did and then I stopped when told to do so. I was then told to turn left (or right—again, I don't exactly remember) and take a certain number of steps. I followed the instructions. A third time I was told to take a few steps in a different direction. When I had completed this and stopped as instructed, I was told to look down and open my eyes. I did. There sat my taw right in front of my feet.

What would you call this? Even if I had somehow seen the marble and it had not registered consciously, how on earth was I able to navigate to it with my eyes closed? You tell me what you think explains this.

There are many other stories I could share and many more that have been shared with me by others. I see this sort of event more as a white crow than knowing without knowing how we know, but whatever it is, the classical mechanistic reductionism offered by those who would debunk anything supernatural simply doesn't have sufficient traction for me.

## Why Does It Matter?

I have just *known* many things in my life. Sometimes I have known where to find a missing animal, or what was in a closed container, and so forth. I have not been able to train this ability to respect my commands, however! Sometimes it's there and sometimes not—but when it's there it has never failed me. That said, it can be exceedingly difficult to know in advance when it's real and when it's not. What does that mean? I honestly can't offer a better explanation than sometimes I must be forcing matters due simply to wishful thinking.

Just as with the train wreck, I don't know what happened. I have been told that there is a phenomenon referred to as tunneling that many people have experienced, as discussed earlier.

This I do know: the message in the train wreck instructed me that there was much more to life than science understood. It may have taken me a while to fully integrate this message, but once I did, I understood something so deep within my being—so necessary, that my prior attitudes toward God and spirituality completely changed.

I was no longer the doubting Thomas or the argumentative antagonist challenging all of those nonsense statements about God, or all of those crazy Biblical passages regarding a jealous and vengeful God, or the selfish implications in stories like that of Job. No, instead I had a deeper need for understanding, and it became, and still is, the driving force in my life.

Chapter 15

# Opining on Enlightenment?

*To know yourself as the Being underneath the thinker, the stillness underneath the mental noise, the love and joy underneath the pain, is freedom, salvation, enlightenment.*
~ Eckhart Tolle

One of the most memorable books that I have ever read is titled *Siddhartha*. This gem of literature was written by Hermann Hesse and won a Pulitzer Prize. It is a wonderful illustration of how we gain enlightenment through living into our selves, living fully into life, and how we cannot become enlightened by listening to an enlightened teacher—we must do it on our own. In the story, Siddhartha finds a river, and there, after traveling afar, learning all there was to be learned from the adepts, indulging in a life of flesh and commerce, enduring the sacrifices of an extreme ascetic, and so forth—there by his river acting now as a simple ferry man for travelers, Siddhartha finds enlightenment. Perhaps his enlightenment began as a result of beholding the awe of nature. We all have been struck with awe in the presence of the astounding power and beauty in nature. And perhaps he allowed himself to stop seeking outside himself for the meaning of life and accepted life for what it is and is not.

### The River

Ever since reading this jewel, I have thought of the river as something each of us must find if we are to become enlightened. In that sense, the river is different for different people. The river lives within all of us. Enlightenment is not about finding the meaning of life by looking outside of yourself, but rather enlightenment comes by simply appreciating the ebb and flow of life's process. Sometimes, the hunt for the river begins as the result of some special event in our lives, but most often the river urges us to discover it by nagging at our instincts, our intuition, and the still small voice within, for it is from within that we chance the opportunity to discover who we really are. This thought has occurred to me several times since my own spiritual path really began. If—and I say *if*—the origination of "all that is" began as the creation epics indicate with God dividing itself, then the spark of that creative force, indeed a piece of it, literally lives with each and every one of us. Given that assumption, it makes sense that if we wish to know God we must first turn within and come to know ourselves—not the conditioned and enculturated self, but our true selves.

There are many forms of denial. One of those that I have often questioned is that attached to what we have selected to believe. How many beliefs do we all have that are the outcrop of some form of denial? For the cigarette smoker who believes smoking will not hurt them because their father smoked for years and lived to be ninety-nine, denial is obviously undergirding their belief. Think of your beliefs—how many of them are possibly derivatives of some form of denial? I wonder if atheism is not one of those denial-based beliefs.

I have spoken with more than a handful of people who have changed their spiritual belief based on a perceived letdown by their understanding of God. The loss of a loved one is a common trigger that can push people away from God. The education system that insists religiosity is nothing more than crude superstitions without any intellectual merit can push the scholar toward accepting this position, else they face discreditation by their peers. Think about your own beliefs—is it possible that some form of denial urged by disappointment or fear of being branded in some negative way has forced you to deny your own experiences?

Chapter 16

# Who Are You?

*Who am I? Not the body, because it is decaying; not the mind,*
*because the brain will decay with the body; not the personality,*
*nor the emotions, for these also will vanish with death.*
~ Ramana Maharshi

There are always reasons, justification, rationalizations, and so
forth for why we are where we are when we wish to make some
change in our lives. Change alone can be scary because it means
giving something up. There was a time when psychological
science insisted that personality was fixed at an early age. Well,
like so many other things that I was taught that have turned out
to be untrue, this one is false as well.

## Authentic Life

I am often asked two questions, "What is an authentic life?"
and, "How does one know whether or not they are living
authentically?"

Sometimes the best way to answer a question is to provide
a clear understanding of its opposite, so what would an
inauthentic life look like? After all, we are living, breathing, and
eating animals, doing natural things, so just what is meant by
living inauthentically?

The quick answer is probably less than satisfying. The quick
answer is living a life untrue to ourselves, but then, what exactly
does that mean? Does it mean that I wanted to be a singer when
I was young and now I'm a scientist instead? Does it mean that
I make a meager wage and therefore I can't live the style I'm
entitled to? Or does it mean something more like: my life is
simply not satisfying, so how could it be authentic?

The Native American Philosopher Lame Deer suggests that an authentic life would not include self-deprecation. Lame Deer believes that we can't stand our natural animal-selves, so we hide from whom we are. We use deodorants and perfumes to hide our smell; we disfigure our faces with cosmetic procedures in desperate attempts to hold aging at bay; we enslave ourselves to a system that reduces us to cogs in the economic machinery; we spend our lives focused on money and define ourselves according to our role in the machination of humanity and thus become not much more than work robots contributing to the never-ending cycle of production and consumption, lost from our true being and from nature itself.

## Consumerism/Modernity

Gandhi believed that modernity was inherently evil and that liberalism, promoting the freedom to do as you please, to make your own consumption decisions, actually made slaves of some in order to benefit others. For Gandhi, the capitalistic industrial complex carried with it the promise of inequitable distribution, and that means the subversion of democracy and the growth of consumerism. The Dalai Lama, like Gandhi, sees consumerism as a pathology.

So, what's wrong with consumerism? After all, the hunt, the chase, the capture — all of this is a part of our primitive makeup, and isn't shopping just our modern sublimation for the good old tribal hunt?

Tolstoy tells us in his work, *The Death of Ivan Ilych*, that for life to be truly meaningful we need to have a connection both with nature and with human relationships. The artificial life, for Tolstoy, is one led in a secular world disconnected from the natural; while devoted to the artificial forms of society that give rise to losing any meaning other than our role in the herd, that leaves us hopeless when the certainty of death draws nigh.

Nietzsche informs us in his *Twilight of the Idols*, that above all, we should always retain our authenticity and take full responsibility for doing so. In his words, "If we possess our why of life, we can put up with any how." He further adds, "The will to a system is a lack of integrity." What he means by that is quite clear. Nietzsche asks us to consider who we are and begs us to evaluate our lives from the maxim of whether we live for ourselves or as some cog in a machine pursuing the goals and purposes of other people. Nietzsche believes that it is our nature to pursue our freedom to rise above and not just be an equal member of the herd.

One of my favorite authors, Og Mandino, compared our modern world and the people that inhabit it to a Nabisco factory. He put it this way: We are no more individual "than any of the millions of saltine crackers that emerge daily."[102]

Lame Deer speaks of the Little Big Horn and General Custer. He narrates a story of how the soldiers under Custer had just been paid and they carried all this paper money, what the Sioux children called "green frog skins." They died for their money, their green frog skins. Those that sent them into battle were doing so for gold in the Black Hills — more green frog skins. The Sioux children used the green frog skins to make toy buffalo and the like. According to Lame Deer, white folks dedicate their lives to green frog skins,[103] and that's why when you ask them who they are, they answer defining their position as a cog in the great machinery: I'm a lawyer, a carpenter, a plumber, a doctor, a truck driver, a waitress, or what have you.

Now, I don't mean to suggest that money is evil. I have a small business, and several people who work for me depend upon their jobs for income, just as my family depends upon me. I hope my employees and associates find their work helping people as rewarding as I do. Still, there are bills to be paid, and we all face that fact every day. So, the real issue is not about those green frog skins, per se, so much as it is about their utility and how much of our lives they define.

## Living Spiritually

Dr. Michael Shermer, the famous agnostic as you may remember (or skeptic as he prefers to describe himself), is the author of *The Believing Brain* and *Why People Believe Weird Things*, among other books. In lucid style, Shermer does an excellent job at describing how and why we are hardwired to want to believe. For Shermer, this represents the foundation explaining how irrational beliefs are formed and reinforced. However, Shermer's list of irrational beliefs includes those traditional explanations and definitions discussed early in this book together with magical events— miracles or white crows as William James put it.

I was once asked a provocative question following a lecture on mind mastery wherein the course clearly demonstrated just how often, and easily, we are manipulated to think and believe the propaganda of the day, whether on behalf of the merchandiser or at the behest of the politician. The question: "What do you believe about religion and spirituality?"

There was a mixed audience of over 200 people, and I knew there would be many belief systems that could easily be tread upon if I was not careful. My personal belief aside, if I was to provide an honest adequate answer to the question, then I knew the answer had to address how we live irrespective of why. I had just interviewed Michael Shermer only a couple of weeks earlier, and his story came to my mind.

When Shermer was younger he was evangelical about his religious faith. He used to go door-to-door preaching the gospel. According to Shermer, it was a friend that got him into religion, and it was his education that ended his involvement. Today, he rather guardedly suggests that he is an agnostic since he is convinced that you can neither prove nor disprove the idea of God. With that said, Shermer has debated many theists including the well-known popular ones such as Deepak Chopra, and often brought his opponent to a state of frustrated anger—a sure indication that they have lost the argument.

Shermer is quick to point out the absurdities such as the idea of an omnipotent or all-powerful god, and therefore the problem with evil. In other words, if God is all-powerful, why is there evil in the world? In fact, if he or she is all-powerful, can they construct a rock so large they cannot lift it?

He loves to draw attention to the idea that if God is all-knowing, omniscient, then there must be no such thing as free will. Everything is known by God and therefore everything is already foreordained.

This is but a small sampling of the approach often taken by Shermer, but he is also quick to draw upon the latest in neuroscience, showing why we believe some of the weird things we believe and how the brain is built to reinforce our beliefs. So, with this additional background on Michael Shermer, let's return to the point—answering the question, "What did I believe about religion and spirituality?"

My answer explained who Michael Shermer was and covered some of our conversation. I had asked Shermer, what was important in life? His response identified his family, neighbors, community, and country as important to him. He felt a duty to his fellow mankind to somehow make their lives lighter, to keep them safe, and to do his part in contributing to the betterment of mankind. In other words, Shermer is the kind of neighbor who would run into your burning house to get you out if he could, and as such, he can be my neighbor anytime!

For me, spirituality and religion are about what you do—not the meetings you attend or the words you use. A spiritual life is lived by way of the actions you take to help others. Ironically, the more you aid another, the more you benefit yourself. For me it is therefore possible to espouse atheism and behave spiritually. That said, as prize-winning physicist Marcelo Gleiser, who won the John Templeton Foundation Award, said, "Atheism is inconsistent with the scientific method." In the words of Gleiser:

To me, science is one way of connecting with the mystery of existence. And if you think of it that way, the mystery of existence is something that we have wondered about ever since people began asking questions about who we are and where we come from. So, while those questions are now part of scientific research, they are much, much older than science. I'm not talking about the science of materials or high-temperature superconductivity, which is awesome and super important, but that's not the kind of science I'm doing. I'm talking about science as part of a much grander and older sort of questioning about who we are in the big picture of the universe. To me, as a theoretical physicist and also someone who spends time out in the mountains, this sort of questioning offers a deeply spiritual connection with the world, through my mind and through my body. Einstein would have said the same thing, I think, with his cosmic religious feeling.[101]

In today's world there is a lot of emphasis on self-esteem. There are all sorts of programs, classes, affirmations, meditations and the like to assist in this area, but nothing can compete with how you feel when you have gone to the aid of another in need and somehow, if only to one person, made a difference. This is how you build true self-esteem—by service to others!

## Creating Personal Icon/Avatar

How do you define your life? If you were to sit down today and create your own avatar, your own icon, and then model it against your being, what character strengths would you assign and what would you change? Would it be outgoing or reserved and cautious? Would you be honest and forthright or secretive and perhaps only selectively honest? Would you be sharing and caring or selfish and self-centered, not just sometimes, but all of the time? Could you be open and friendly, or do you need your space and feel somewhat introverted? The real question then is, if you were to choose, to genuinely become your own architect of your character, your personality, would you be different in any way? And if so, how?

How about religiosity? Would you be more spiritual, or would you be more inclined to defer the idea of life after death and seek to satisfy the carnal desires of the moment? If you recognize anything it should be that you either choose that your life ends and that's it—from dust to dust—or there just might be the possibility that who you ultimately are continues in some realm to exist. If you choose that this possibility exists, then one must recognize that the things in our life will not accompany us into the afterlife. What will remain with us is our memories and our relationships. I know it feels good to believe that there is an afterlife and that we may well be able to be with our loved ones on the other side—and why shouldn't it feel grand? Bottom line, if you create that avatar, create it with this in mind.

# Chapter 17

# Living Wisely

*It is impossible to live a pleasant life*
*without living wisely and well and justly.*
*And it is impossible to live wisely and well and justly*
*without living a pleasant life.*
~ Epicurus

There are many things that we can do to live more wisely. Once we become conscious of the many mechanisms that are either a part of the architecture of homo sapiens and/or the result of our enculturation and socialization, we have the power to preempt these mechanisms. Unfortunately, it really does take a wholehearted and fully aware perspective to effectively mitigate their control over much of our lives.

Habits can be powerful. I once attended an addiction CEU course where the instructor found himself having one of those inner dialogues where our desire convinces our better judgment to take a back seat. Despite his conscious determination to avoid donuts in order to lose some truly excessive weight, he nevertheless found himself wheeling into *Krispy Kreme* almost automatically. Well obviously, to most it is easy to find ourselves doing exactly the opposite of what we know is best. That's not to provide anyone with an excuse, including myself, but rather to illustrate how easy it is to be fooled by ourselves. I was hungry and so I was vulnerable and ergo—"well, I'll do better next time" might be our pledge.

Sometimes that inner commitment to do better next time is the best thing we can do, and never underestimate its power. We have acquired our habits and mechanisms over a lifetime.

Changing them can sometimes be a slow but accumulative process — emphasis on accumulative.

Over our lifetimes we build beliefs, habits, interests, and so forth. Some of these serve us and some fail. Much of who we are exists in the sub world of our subconscious mind. Our defense mechanisms and strategies are unconscious by definition until we make them conscious. As such, the process of getting to know ourselves, our true selves, is definitely a true journey, and as important as it is to undertake this journey is our willingness to accept what we find.

## Mistakes

It is natural for almost everyone to think of himself or herself as basically a good person. Sometimes what we find discourages this view by revealing thoughts, feelings, and actions we become ashamed of as we move along our path of self-knowledge. I certainly know this is true for me. I can think of mistakes I have made that at the time I fully justified. I can be humiliated by some of them today, and that feeling makes me want to shove the memory aside or justify it in some way. For example, when I was teenager riding with a friend in his car, we picked up a hitchhiker we both knew. He was our age and attended the same high school. He was a good Mormon, and I was smoking. He wanted to know why I smoked, and he wanted me to put the cigarette out. So, I gripped his hand and extinguished the cigarette in his palm. Obviously, I was angered by his religious attitude, and as you know by now, thoroughly disgusted with the Mormon faith. Where I may have justified this at the time, today I am deeply ashamed and disgusted with myself. My action was that of a punk, or what so many in law enforcement refer to as a scumbag. Pure and simple—I was wrong—oh so wrong!

I wish this was the only time I could remember that I made huge mistakes, but it's not. All I can say is, "I'm truly sorry!"

Sorry doesn't fix things but it may lead to forgiving myself, and I hope I am eventually forgiven by all whom I have harmed in some way. What I must do is accept what I did and who I was before I can become a better person. I must also learn to forgive myself, but I can only do that if and only if I do indeed become a better person.

So goes the journey of true self-discovery. So goes the path of enlightenment. And so goes the way to inner-truth and strength. Why is this important? Because if there is an afterlife, what I fail to recognize and reconcile in this life will undoubtedly overwhelm me in the next. Additionally, forgiveness unlocks the prison that otherwise holds me captive.

## Chapter 18

# Nine Exercises that Change Lives

*Change your thoughts and you change your world.*
~ Norman Vincent Peale

I like to close all my books with tools and practices that can improve lives. To that end, a question I have often been asked can be paraphrased this way: "What can I do to become more aware, more awake, and enhance the quality of my life in doing so?" This chapter is dedicated to sorting out some of the most obvious and easiest methods that can be deployed for just this purpose. Whether you have chosen a spiritual or secular path, the following techniques and exercises are pragmatic for all.

### Number One: Each Morning Upon Awakening

This tip is really powerful and oh so simple. When you first open your eyes in the morning, take a deep breath, smile, and speak aloud, thank you, thank you, thank you! This simple little procedure can change your life. The smile triggers the brain and those good feeling chemicals, the endorphins, the body's natural opiates are released. The thank you puts a spin on the day, one of gratitude. Instead of thinking about all you might have in front of you that you would rather not have to deal with, your thoughts shift to the good things before you. This optimism shifts your perspective, and that has been proven to have both positive health benefits and the winning way that prevails in all forms of success from relationships to business.

Taking that deep breath fills your lungs with oxygen, and like priming a pump, it leads to rapidly awakening and energizing your system. I add this affirmation every morning, modifying some an idea original with the French psychologist and pharmacist, Émile Coué, saying very meaningfully to myself: "Every day in every way I improve!"

## Number Two: Sing for Ten Minutes

Research has shown that simply singing each day for ten minutes will improve your attitude and your health, bringing a calming effect to your being. In fact, choir practice has been shown to be healthier than yoga. Singing trains our lungs to breathe better, boosts our immune system, reduces stress levels and manages pain. According to a study conducted at Yale University in 2008, singing increases your life expectancy.[105]

## Number Three: Sa Ta Na Ma Meditation

During a Hay House Summit conversation, I discussed the twelve-minute meditation practice that the data showed had an amazing effect on cognitive abilities. Many people wrote me about this exercise. This simple exercise not only increases cognitive abilities, but it also actually rewires the brain. It takes only twelve minutes a day and is a secular practice. This is a particularly powerful practice not just for the cognitive improvements, but like all meditation, it increases our mindfulness while producing all the other great health benefits associated with meditation.

This is the twelve-minute practice I'm referring to, and you may remember that we discussed it some earlier. You are to use four intonations, the mantra: sa, ta, na, ma. You are going to enunciate the four intonations accompanied by a simple mudra. The mudra requires touching your forefinger to your thumb, then your middle finger to your thumb, then your ring finger, and finally your little finger. So, you will say, sa while you touch your forefingers to your thumbs, using both hands for this practice. Then it's ta and the next finger, and so forth. So, you're going to repeat sa, ta, na, ma; sa, ta, na, ma; and so forth in your normal voice for two minutes. You will then continue with the same mudra and mantra whispering it to yourself for two more minutes. Then for four minutes you will silently proceed to repeat the mantra while continuing with the mudra. Then it's two more minutes whispering and finally two more minutes spoken in normal voice and the practice is complete.

I can remember a friend of mine, the former chief of police of a city in Utah, learning that I meditated. Now this was back in the early 1980s, and I received quite a bit of ribbing about meditation from him and others on the force. They wanted to lump me in with the Hari Krishnas hanging out in the airports and handing out pamphlets, and no self-respecting member of law enforcement or their ilk desired to be labeled in this way. Well, the pendulum swings; today health care professionals recommend meditation for a variety of reasons. One of the first recommendations a cardiac care patient will receive will include some sort of meditation practice. The bottom line is simple: meditation is for everyone—literally everyone!

## Number Four: Remember the Positive
Taking just twenty minutes a day to reflect/remembering the positive moments in your life can lift your mood. Mood states can have a strong influence on our health. Feeling gloomy has potentially more than psychological implications. Depression can lead to serious health disadvantages just the same as continual heightened states of arousal. One of the best mood fixers exists in this tip. Take twenty minutes out of your day, perhaps while you enjoy lunch, to reminisce over the good memories. Think about your favorite happy moments, dwell on those for twenty minutes, and you'll find you feel enriched by the procedure.

## Number Five: Laugh and Laugh Some More
Laughter is much better for you than you might think. Norman Cousins, in his book *Anatomy of an Illness*, insisted that he

healed himself of cancer using laughter. Consciously choosing to take part of your day to watch or read something hilarious is participating in consciously choosing to add laughter to your every day.

There are many health benefits to laughing to say nothing of the psychological advantages to feeling happy. The body basically has two budgets analogous to a government. One is for defense and the other for growth. When we allow stressors to lead to defense, such as when we get upset or become angry, or feel slighted or dissed, and so forth, for that matter, whenever we experience anxiety, our defenses become dominant, and the body is flooded with all of those neurochemicals including adrenaline that inhibit the optimal operation of our immune, endocrine, and autonomic nervous system. When we are laughing and having fun, the opposite is true. All of those good neurochemicals are facilitating growth.

Laughter has been shown to stimulate organs, strengthen the immune system, reduce pain, and improve blood pressure among its many benefits.[106] So, set some time off every day to laugh hard—consider it part of your daily exercise regime.

## Number Six: Be Ingratiating

This one may surprise many, but it is a healthy practice to pass sincere compliments around every day. Not only does it make others feel good, but it also helps you in a variety of ways. Indeed, there are books on how to use ingratiation as a tactic to control or influence others. Setting that aside, the reason ingratiation is included here is the simple fact that acknowledging the good in others lifts your own spirits and leads to the recognition of good within yourself.

This is not the practice of shallow flattery. In order to be truly ingratiating, you must be observant. This causes you to begin to search for good in everyone. When you are able to see good in all, you may begin to see the Divine spark that is the life force in each of us.

It's easy to find good in good people, but how about those for whom we hold no kind words? There are many practices that inform us that what we resist in others is something we resist in ourselves. In other words, the world is a mirror unto each and all of us. When we can appreciate the least within ourselves, we are able to love the least within another. Within every man or woman is the infant, with so much potential, that they once were. Someone loves everyone. Find the good and point it out, and in this way, you encourage more of it.

Remember, this practice must be sincere, and it does not imply accepting or approving of everyone. Acknowledging the good in one is not the same as condoning their actions. I can recognize the commitment one holds and even their willingness to sacrifice in the name of their cause, and still disagree with both their cause and their actions.

## Number Seven: Do A Good Deed

Doing a good deed and keeping a journal is something I have been encouraging people to do ever since I learned the power of this simple practice. I have seen clinically depressed patients completely end depression as a result of using this one simple trick. It is the best way I know to learn just how much value you are capable of bringing to our world, and therefore just how important you are to all of us. Now when you journal your good deeds, be sure to reflect on just how it made you feel to go to the aid of someone in need. I promise this will elevate your sense of well-being in every dimension.

## Number Eight: Choose to Emulate

This practice is not the hardest to do and may be the one most procrastinated. Choose a personality to emulate. When we were children, we did this all of the time. We used to rehearse everything. Most of us stood in front of the mirror from time to time and practiced looks, mannerisms, comments, and even speeches. I am familiar with a person who kissed his pillow more than a hundred times, all in preparation to kiss his first girlfriend.

The fact is, we are made with mirror neurons. These specialized neurons make it easy for us to copy behavior. Mirror neurons are activated and fire, both when they see an action of another animal and when they perform the same action. Observing a behavior, an act, elicits differing responses from mirror neurons. You may witness someone stumble and fall and find yourself flinching. You may view a movie and become involved in some action scene as though you were actually there. Mirror neurons are thought to be involved with empathy as well as mimicry.

Remember that the philosopher Friedrich Nietzsche suggested in his essay on values that we both voluntarily and consciously choose our characteristics. Indeed, he asks the question, "Why don't we?"

Most of us are the result of our enculturation, and just as our native tongue is inherited, so are most of our personal characteristics. Everything about us has been patterned by our nature/nurture environment. From the way we walk to the way we talk, the things we admire and those that disgust us — our every attribute has been modeled from something we have processed with our senses.

When you give this serious thought, you realize that even your thoughts are secondhand. It takes serious effort and time to find a truly original thought that we have ever had in our lives, if we find one at all. So given this understanding, why would we not want to sit down and become our own architects?

So, step eight is a very straightforward exercise. Make a list of characteristics about yourself that you would like to emulate, as discussed earlier. Do you want to be more patient? Would you like to be admired for your honesty? Would you like to be more outgoing, have a better sense of humor, be more daring and courageous, possess better habits, and so forth? Make a list of what you desire and then match it with behavior. You can do that by choosing someone to act as your icon. If you admire someone, copy them. John Paul Getty once remarked something like, the way to success is to copy success. So, choose your icon or icons. Perhaps you have one icon who represents a behavior you wish and another who represents some other behavior or facet of behavior you are desirous of owning.

You can also do this by simply visualizing the sort of action necessary in order to achieve your goals. Now a word of advice regarding this method: instead of thinking about those matters you wish to change, think about those you wish to acquire. Let's say you are ashamed of how often you lie or fabricate or exaggerate. Think of how someone who never did this sort of thing would behave. Think of the courage it sometimes takes to be honest and begin to behave accordingly. It is far easier to extinguish an unwanted behavior by behaving in a mutually exclusive manner than it is to argue and debate with yourself about the behavior, and that is generally what happens when you think about the motives behind the behavior.

## Number Nine: Likeability

There are health benefits to being likable. Your likeability, or what has been called your "L" factor, can be key to your success in all walks of life. Research has demonstrated that more than performance, it is your L factor that is likely to determine your promotion at work. Your L factor is obviously important when it comes to personal relationships but less well recognized is its importance when it comes to your overall well-being. There are direct links to depression and other stress-related illnesses that have been causally connected to a low L factor.

There are several things that one can do to increase their L factor. The first is begin by smiling. Smile whenever you greet someone. Make a sincere smile of warmth. Think about it.

Likable people make other people feel good, feel important, feel liked! A warm ingratiating smile covers a multitude of sins!

Develop empathy. You can do that by simply putting yourself in others' shoes. Listen to others and engage them in ways that help you understand their situation so you can begin to relate. When others feel that you understand them, or at the very least, are trying to do so, they respect you and your likability grows.

Think about others. What can you do to show them you care? Offer to assist them when possible. If you can cheer someone up, your L factor will grow with them exponentially.

Develop a sense of humor. Often L factors are based on not much more than having fun. Fun people know how to laugh including how to laugh at themselves.

Avoid gossip. Let everyone know that you don't participate in gossip. Be warm and friendly with those who you warn away regarding gossip, with something reassuring like, "You know—I just make it a practice not to gossip or participate in it." Then change the subject and engage the person in a new conversation.

Building your L factor takes time. Be patient and persevere.

Some of the behaviors I am recommending here may reveal to you a spirituality that lives within. For me, as I indicated earlier, what's important about spirituality is not what you say, where you go to church, the book you hold up as your authority, and so forth—no, what's truly spiritual is how you live. From my perspective, living your life in accordance with the plan set out in this chapter is living a spiritual life.

# Chapter 19

# Conclusion

*Very little is needed to make a happy life;*
*it is all within yourself, in your way of thinking.*
~ Marcus Aurelius

So, what are we to think? Perhaps the answer is in the question—we are to think! It may be convenient at times to take shortcuts, but these same shortcuts can short-circuit our reasoning ability. Webster defines convenience as, "The state of being able to proceed with something with little effort or difficulty." Now we all like our conveniences and why shouldn't we? But this is not the sort of convenient that I want to address. No, the class of convenient I have in mind is that story, that explanation, that response that conveniently explains an otherwise difficult topic. This sort of convenient comes in at least two forms.

Perhaps a couple of examples will help unpack what I am suggesting. The first form comes in what I think of as an evasive way. Imagine a conversation where someone makes a statement that is clearly untrue, and you challenge it. They respond with something like this, "Well, I was told that, so I don't really know for sure." Now that's a convenient way to duck a lie—but perhaps they were actually told it by someone, so they get a pass. After all, the nature of their convenient response "might" be true.

So, you pursue this. "Who told you that?" Their answer: "I don't remember." Again, how convenient, but then, there is no penalty for forgetting so once again they get a free pass. Oh, you might shrug and think to yourself, "How convenient," but then that's usually the end of it unless you're being cross-examined in a court of law.

I seem to have been in the business of interviewing folks for most of my life. I have interviewed more than a thousand during criminal investigations or lie detection scenarios, and several hundred more on my radio shows—and that doesn't include the hundred plus that I have interviewed as an employer. I have often come to expect "convenient answers" when the subject gets dicey.

## Credibility

Not long ago we hosted Dan Ariely on *Provocative Enlightenment Radio*. Ariely is a professor of psychology and behavioral economics teaching at Duke University. He is the founder of the Center for Advanced Hindsight and the author *Predictably Irrational* and *The (Honest) Truth About Dishonesty*. His research tells a compelling story: we all lie!

Now to an honest person, that doesn't come as any surprise. Some make a career out of it—that is, at least out of exaggeration and what advertising attorneys call "puffing." Politicians are famous for lies and broken promises and "convenient answers." So, what's the big deal?

Credibility—that's the big deal! We live in a world where the truth is often in shorter supply than water in the Mojave. How do we know what to believe? Does everyone have an agenda? Is everything about selling us a product, an idea, a way of thinking, etc.?

I can choose almost any subject and find contrary information. Recent headlines told stories of the not-so-well-known ingredients in vaccines, such as formaldehyde, and how we should avoid many. Turn the page and you might read where recommendations to make it criminal if you either bad-mouth vaccines or refuse to get yours have been proposed. Obviously, we must all be alert to the agendas on both sides of arguments, but should we also challenge the seeming incredible statements offered by many in the name of spirituality? Well, I think so!

Take, for example, this one as what I referred to as a second type of convenient nonsense. Once I interviewed a person who had belonged to a church that prepared for the end of the world. It was certain and it was near, so they built special shelters, put in food and water, and so forth. When the day was close at hand, the members descended into their bunkers to await Armageddon. A few days later they cautiously surfaced to find everything as it was—no Armageddon. How did they explain this? The answer is simple, obviously their efforts, their goodness, their prayers averted the tragedy. Unlike the days of Noah or Lot, there apparently were more than enough good people to spare the earth. Now that's a downright convenient answer in my view.

The world today has developed science and technology that surpasses any time in history. We possess the ability to clone a human being, to make decisions with artificial intelligence, to view the operation of the brain live time and map its processes, to modify the DNA molecule and so much more, and yet, we still have a world full of superstition and nonsense. I am sometimes reminded of the fourteenth through seventeenth centuries—a time in history when tens of thousands of witches were killed. This was going on during the lives of men like Galileo, Bacon, and Newton. Indeed, the great renaissance of art and architecture as well as science blossomed during this period. How then, in retrospect, did folks go so wrong searching out and killing witches?

I would implore you, when you hear hoof beats—think horses first, not Centaurs. And when you get that convenient answer—don't be rude but don't dismiss it either! At the same time, don't just accept some dogmatic answer because you like how it makes you feel or worse yet, because most people believe it! Science has many dogmatists, but how then can they truly be scientists, for science is all about enquiry and dogmatism has no room for that.

## Waking Up

We wake up one person at a time and waking up requires the careful discrimination of information you use to guide your way in what can seem like a confusing and sometimes dark world. We all would like to escape the dark whenever we encounter it but running to any old light will only end in disappointment and more darkness.

In the end, we shall all either find our life after or not. Many of the benefits gained from living a spiritual life may well be obtainable without a belief in a hereafter. We have discussed three reasonable rationales for living spiritually—and they are by way of practical reasoning, the pragmatic, and the white crows.

Now, by way of clarification, I in no way mean to conflate reason with rationale. Sometimes a rationale can be rational, but there are instances where a rationale is nothing more than an excuse. I say this in order to raise the question: are your reasons rational or are they just convenient forms of an excuse—a rationale, for what you choose to believe and/or behave? We should all examine this question when applying the construct of pragmatics.

I have tried to present both sides of the argument while leaving the real synthesis to you. We each must find our own rivers, and that is my wish for you.

# Afterword

*It's asking that never-ending question, "Who am I?"*
*which motivates me and takes me on a constant journey*
*of self-discovery that teaches me so much.*
~ Ant Middleton

Gordon Brown, former prime minister of the UK, stated, "Our common realm is not and cannot be stripped of values—I absolutely reject the idea that religion should somehow be tolerated but not encouraged in public life."[107] The purpose of this work was and is simple—to demonstrate that it simply is *not irrational* to believe in an afterlife or higher power. In my mind, I have met that challenge. Spirituality is not the domain of the so-called unintelligent, superstitious, uneducated, and so forth. I sincerely hope that you have come to recognize the inherent advantages in living spiritually, but more importantly than that, I hope you choose to live a life that contributes to your own self-actualization.

I wish you the very best in your every endeavor, and I'm grateful for your feedback. You can write me at eldon@eldontaylor.com or join me on Facebook at DrEldonTaylor.

# Appendix A

Some of my readers suggested that I took the reader too deep into the hole when it came to presenting the thesis of the atheist. One reader put it this way, "My concern is that in drawing out your sons in the manner that you have, you may create the exact opposite result that you intend." Another reader suggested that my sons are presently atheists, and my efforts are obviously in vain. I don't know how I communicated that, but the fact is neither have remained atheistic, in large due to the many hours of discussion that formed the framework for this book. As such, I felt it necessary to dispel this potential misunderstanding by adding some clarification including the following, written by my son, William. I continue to believe that it is important to meet the atheist on their own turf, so to speak, and demonstrate that you understand their thinking, arguments, and concerns. It is only by approaching the discussion in this manner that you may gain any traction toward them accepting the idea that it is as rational to believe in some higher power as it is not.

Here are my son's thoughts on *Questioning Spirituality*:
As the title might suggest, my father's newest book is a conversation on spirituality—whether it's rational or irrational to believe in a god and what we have to gain, or lose, in so doing. Of course, my father's idea is what it always has been—it is far more rational to believe than not to believe. And, of course, we're naturally primed to believe in a god of some kind. We've always ascribed to the supernatural what we can't explain; as Arthur C. Clarke said, "Any sufficiently advanced technology is indistinguishable from magic." We have also aggressively asserted that the stronger of the supernaturals was inherently good.

In Greek Mythos, that dichotomy is easily portrayed as Zeus, Poseidon, and Hades. Hades, being equitable with darkness, pain, suffering, and death, is routinely defeated by the other two gods—Zeus with the sky, and lightning, and Poseidon with the tides and the oceans. For a coastal empire, it is particularly easy to understand the fear and awe of Zeus and Poseidon. Hades of course simply inspires fear. This tendency is universal, even when our own "religious evidence" begs to differ.

For example, I went to a Catholic high school, and it wasn't at all uncommon for me to hear from my more religious classmates or teachers that they "feared their god", but that they trusted that their god had a plan for them and loved them. That never sat right with me. Love and fear are opposites. "Fear and having a plan" is considerably more sinister than "love and having a plan." But they would swear by it, prickle at it being questioned, and finally end with something like my father's "refrain from the mysteries." Personally, my favorite was always, "You can't begin to understand the machinations of god. He is incomprehensible to you. You just have to have faith."

The strength of this book, at its core, is that it doesn't refrain from anything. While I don't necessarily agree with every point, I can recognize it and appreciate it for what it is—a discussion. It makes you consider your perspectives, and those counter to them, regardless of which side of that aisle you may fall on. And I deeply appreciate it for that.

Honestly, reading this book felt as close to sitting in my father's dining room in Spokane as the sun sets, drinking a glass of whisky, and talking in those big, vague, curious terms you often get to after one too many. It felt like a discussion where you're free to interject your own thoughts, opinions, and talking points as you see fit. The book leaves room for it.

Of course, I'd be remiss if I didn't point out the irony in its writing. That is, when my father originally decided to write the book, I was a freshman in college. I was finally free of that aforementioned Catholic high school, and God damn did I hate the idea of religion. I was attending the University of Washington in Seattle—the most aggressively secular place I've ever experienced—and I was embracing it as an excuse. Of course, this all reads as an excuse too, now that I write it, but my point is that of course I was atheistic.

However, a lot's changed in the last five years. I've grown, graduated, experienced that "real world" my parents kept telling me about, had many conversations, and my opinions have changed. That is, this book has been in the works for so long that my stance has changed. I'm not an atheist anymore, if only because I find myself hoping to the same ethereal supernatural as you would be as you set sail from Mykonos in 200 BCE.

So, in one way or another, Dad, you've already achieved success in your introduction's goal. Not bad for the book not yet being published yet, huh?

# Endnotes

1.  Fairbanks, E. 2019. "Behold the Millennial Nuns." *HuffPost.* https://www.huffpost.com/highline/article/millennial-nuns/
2.  Toscano, P.J. 1979. "A Dubious Neutrality: The Establishment of Secularism in the Public Schools." *BYU Law Review*, Vol. 1979, Issue 2, Article 1. https://digitalcommons.law.byu.edu/cgi/viewcontent.cgi?article=1191&context=lawreview
3.  Grabmeier, J. 2013. "False Beliefs Persist, Even After Instant Online Corrections." *The Ohio State University*. January 24, 2013. https://news.osu.edu/false-beliefs-persist-even-after-instant-online-corrections/
4.  Asch, S.E. 1951. "Effects of group pressure on the modification and distortion of judgments." In H. Guetzkow (Ed.), *Groups, leadership and men* (pp. 177-190). Pittsburgh, PA: Carnegie Press.
5.  Showalter, E. 1997. *Hystories: Hysterical Epidemics and Modern Culture*. West Sussex, UK: Columbia University Press.
6.  Shermer, M. 2004. "God's Number is Up." *Michael Shermer*. https://michaelshermer.com/sciam-columns/gods-number-is-up/
7.  Libet, B., Alberts, W.W., and Wright, E.W. 1976. "Responses of Human Somatosensory Cortex to Stimuli Below Threshold for Conscious Sensation." *Science*, 158 (3808), 1597-1600.
8.  Smith, K. 2011. "Neuroscience vs philosophy: Taking Aim at Free Will." *Nature*, 477, 23-2.
9.  Keim, B. 2008. "Brain Scanners Can See Your Decisions Before You Make Them." *Wired*. April 13, 2008. https://www.wired.com/2008/04/mind-decision/ and

Soon, C.S., Brass, M., Heinze, H.J., & Haynes, J.D. "Unconscious determinants of free decisions in the human brain." *Nature Neuroscience.* http://citeseerx.ist.psu.edu/viewdoc/download?doi=10.1.1.520.2204&rep=rep1&type=pdf

10. – 2010. "Free Will." *Stanford Encyclopedia of Philosophy Archive.* Summer 2016 edition. https://plato.stanford.edu/archives/sum2016/entries/freewill/

11. – "What is Epigenetics?" *Medline Plus.* https://medlineplus.gov/genetics/understanding/howgeneswork/epigenome/

12. Hayasaki, E. 2018. "Identical Twins Hint at How Environments Change Gene Expression." *The Atlantic.* May 15, 2018. https://www.theatlantic.com/science/archive/2018/05/twin-epigenetics/560189/

13. Ibid

14. Hughes, V. 2014. "Epigenetics: The sins of the father." *Nature,* 507, 22-24. March 5, 2014. https://www.nature.com/articles/507022a

15. Ibid

16. RMIT University. "Sins of the father could weigh on the next generation." *ScienceDaily.* ScienceDaily, 1 December 2015. https://www.sciencedaily.com/releases/2015/12/151201113925.htm

and

Govic, A., Penman, J., Tammer, A.H., and Paolini, A.G. 2016. "Paternal calorie restriction prior to conception alters anxiety-like behavior of the adult rat progeny." *Psychoneuroendocrinology,* 2016; 64.

17. – "Scientists Identify Genes Associated with Violent Crime." *IFL Science.* https://www.iflscience.com/brain/genes-associated-violent-crimes-identified/

18. Dawkins, R. 1976. *The Selfish Gene.* Oxford University Press.

19. Lewis, T. 2014. "Twins Separated at Birth Reveal Staggering Influence of Genetics." *Live Science.* August 11, 2014.

20. Freud, S. 1927. *The Future of an Illusion.*
21. Mele, A. "Neuroscience and Free Will." *Philosophy, Science and Religion: Science and Philosophy. Coursera.* https://www.coursera.org/lecture/philosophy-science-religion-1/introduction-4DgEJ
22. – "Predeterminism." Wikipedia. https://en.wikipedia.org/wiki/Predeterminism
23. Newberg, A. 2012. *The Spiritual Brain: Science and Religious Experience. Great Courses.*
24. Ibid
25. Association for Psychological Science. 2013. "Experiencing awe increases belief in the supernatural." *Cognitive Science.* November 26, 2013. https://www.psypost.org/2013/11/experiencing-awe-increases-belief-in-the-supernatural-21428
    and
    – 2013. "Experiencing awe increases belief in the supernatural." (e) *Science News.* November 25, 2013. https://esciencenews.com/articles/2013/11/25/experiencing.awe.increases.belief.supernatural
26. Association for Psychological Science. 2013. "Experiencing awe increases belief in the supernatural." *Cognitive Science.* November 26, 2013. https://www.psypost.org/2013/11/experiencing-awe-increases-belief-in-the-supernatural-21428
    and
    https://esciencenews.com/articles/2013/11/25/experiencing.awe.increases.belief.supernatural
27. Newberg, A. 2012. *The Spiritual Brain: Science and Religious Experience. Great Courses.*
28. Ibid
29. Hamer, Dean H. 2004. *The God Gene.* NY: Anchor.
30. Zimmer, C. 2004. "Faith-Boosting Genes." *Scientific American.* October 31, 2004.

31. Newberg, A. 2012. *The Spiritual Brain: Science and Religious Experience. Great Courses.*
32. Ibid
33. Ibid
34. Ibid
35. Ibid
36. Hamer, Dean H. 2004. *The God Gene.* NY: Anchor.
37. Dawkins, R. 1976. *The Selfish Gene.* Oxford University Press.
38. Moss, A.S. et al. 2012. "Effects Of An 8-Week Meditation Program on Mood and Anxiety in Patients with Memory Loss." *J Altern Complement Med,* 2012 Jan;18(1):48-53.
39. Heffernan, M. 2011. *Willful Blindness: Why We Ignore the Obvious at Our Peril.* Walker Books.
40. Shortell, D. 2019. "Barr slams attacks on religious values, says 'moral upheaval' leading to societal ills." CNN. October 12, 2019. https://www.cnn.com/2019/10/12/politics/william-barr-religious-values-moral-upheaval/index.html
41. Douthat, R. 2007. "Secularism and Marxism." *The Atlantic.* June 15, 2007. https://www.theatlantic.com/personal/archive/2007/06/secularism-and-marxism/54482/
42. Rand, A. 1957. *Atlas Shrugged.* Random House.
43. Hitchens, C. 2007. *God Is Not Great: How Religion Poisons Everything.* Twelve Books.
44. Charles, E. 2014. "Atheism is Irrational." *Psychology Today.* February 14, 2014. https://www.psychologytoday.com/us/blog/fixing-psychology/201402/atheism-is-irrational
45. Ibid
46. Billings, L. 2019. "Atheism Is Inconsistent with the Scientific Method, Prizewinning Physicist Says." *Scientific American.* March 20, 2019.
47. Editors. "Steady-State Theory." Britannica. https://www.britannica.com/science/steady-state-theory
48. Carter, J.A. et al. *Philosophy, Science and Religion: Science and Philosophy. Coursera.*

49. – "Practical Reason and Theoretical." *Science Encyclopedia.* https://science.jrank.org/pages/10997/Reason-Practical-Theoretical-Definitions-Relationships.html

50. Kaufman, S.B. 2015. "Which Character Strengths Are Most Predictive of Well-Being?" *Scientific American Blogs.* August 2, 2015. https://blogs.scientificamerican.com/beautiful-minds/which-character-strengths-are-most-predictive-of-well-being/

51. Cherry, K. 2021. "What Is Learned Helplessness and Why Does it Happen?" *Very Well Mind.* April 5, 2021. https://www.verywellmind.com/what-is-learned-helplessness-2795326

52. Richter, C.P. 1957. "On the phenomenon of sudden death in animals and man." *Psychosomatic Medicine*, 19, 191-8. and
Hallinan, J.T. 2014. "The Remarkable Power of Hope." *Psychology Today.* May 7, 2014. https://www.psychologytoday.com/us/blog/kidding-ourselves/201405/the-remarkable-power-hope

53. Stern, S.L., Dhanda, R., & Hazuda, H.P. 2001. "Hopelessness Predicts Mortality in Older Mexican and European Americans." *Psychosomatic Medicine*, 63:344-351.

54. Everson, S.A. et al. 1996. "Hopelessness and Risk of Mortality and Incidence of Myocardial Infarction and Cancer." *Psychosomatic Medicine*, Mar-Apr 1996;58(2):113-21. https://pubmed.ncbi.nlm.nih.gov/8849626/

55. Gilman, S.E. et al. 2017. "Depression and Mortality in a Longitudinal Study: 1952-2011." *CMA Journal*, Oct 23;189(42).

56. Sevensky, R.L. 1981. "Religion and Illness: An Outline of Their Relationship." *South Med J.*, Jun;74(6):745-50. https://pubmed.ncbi.nlm.nih.gov/7244757/

57. Smith, C. 2012. "The Science of Smiling: The Anatomy and Function of a Smile." *Visible Body.* Sept. 17, 2012. https://www.visiblebody.com/blog/learn-the-science-behind-a-smile-visualized-with-visible-body

58. Ibid

59. Brown, J. & Wong, J. 2017. "How Gratitude Changes You and Your Brain." *Greater Good Magazine*. June 6, 2017. https://greatergood.berkeley.edu/article/item/how_gratitude_changes_you_and_your_brain

60. Khan, S. 2019. "Scientists Say That Gratitude Alters the Heart and Molecular Structure of the Brain." *The Science Times*. November 26, 2019. https://www.sciencetimes.com/articles/24318/20191126/mental-health.htm

61. Demeter, F. 2015. "2 Words That Will Change Your Life: Thank You." *Crosswalk*. November 21, 2015. https://www.crosswalk.com/faith/bible-study/2-words-that-will-change-your-life-thank-you.html

62. Scott, E. 2020. "What is Spirituality?" *Very Well Mind*. November 27, 2020. https://www.verywellmind.com/how-spirituality-can-benefit-mental-and-physical-health-3144807

63. Seppälä, E. 2016. "The Surprising Health Benefits of Spirituality." *Psychology Today*. August 8, 2016. https://www.psychologytoday.com/us/blog/feeling-it/201608/the-surprising-health-benefits-spirituality

64. Ibid

65. Florida State University. 2013. "Power of Prayer: Studies Find Prayer Can Lead to Cooperation, Forgiveness in Relationships." *ScienceDaily*. 14 May 2013.

66. Sharp, S. 2010. "How Does Prayer Help Manage Emotions?" *Social Psychology Quarterly*, 2010; 73 (4): 417.

67. Association for Psychological Science. 2010. "Prayer Increases Forgiveness, Study Shows." *ScienceDaily*. 1 February 2010.

68. Ibid

69. Scott, E. 2020. "What is Spirituality?" *Very Well Mind*. November 27, 2020. https://www.verywellmind.com/how-spirituality-can-benefit-mental-and-physical-health-3144807

70. Ibid
71. Buettner, D. "Reverse Engineering Longevity." *Blue Zones.* https://www.bluezones.com/2016/11/power-9/
72. Pappas, S. 2012. "8 Ways Religion Impacts Your Life." *Live Science.* February 19, 2012. https://www.livescience. com/18421-religion-impacts-health.html
73. Staff. 2011. "Happiness & Health." *Harvard School of Public Health.* https://www.hsph.harvard.edu/news/magazine/ happiness-stress-heart-disease/
74. Ibid
75. Newberg, A. 2012. *The Spiritual Brain: Science and Religious Experience. Great Courses.*
76. Muller, R.J. 2008. "Neurotheology: Are We Hardwired for God?" *Psychiatric Times*, Vol 25, No. 6, Issue 6. https:// www.psychiatrictimes.com/view/neurotheology-are-we-hardwired-god
77. Ibid
78. Ibid
79. – "Pragmatism." *Internet Encyclopedia of Philosophy.* https:// iep.utm.edu/pragmati/
80. Manglos, N.D. 2013. "Faith Pinnacle Moments: Stress, Miraculous Experiences, and Life Satisfaction in Young Adulthood." *Sociology of Religion*, Volume 74, Issue 2, Summer 2013, pp. 176-198.
81. Taylor, E. 2012. *I Believe: When What You Believe Matters.* Carlsbad, CA: Hay House.
82. Staff. 1998. "Church Explosion Spares Choir." *Snopes.* December 31, 1998. https://www.snopes.com/fact-check/ choir-non-quorum/
83. Logan, K. "Communication Possible Between Minds Separated by Distance." *Forever Conscious.* https:// foreverconscious.com/communication-possible-between-minds-separated-by-distance

84. University of Washington. 2019. "How You and Your Friends Can Play a Video Game Together Using Only Your Minds." *ScienceDaily.* 1 July 2019.

85. Tressoldi, P. et al. 2014. "Brain-To-Brain (Mind-To-Mind) Interaction at Distance: A Confirmatory Study." *F1000 Research.* https://f1000research.com/articles/3-182

86. Tymn, M. 2015. *The Articulate Dead: They Brought the Spirit World Alive.* Galde Press.

87. Root, C. 2019. "The Bridey Murphy Saga: Yesterday's News Vol. V." *Denver Library Newsletter.* October 22, 2019. https://history.denverlibrary.org/news/bridey-murphy-saga-yesterdays-news-vol-v

88. Laszlo, E. & Peake, A. 2014. *The Immortal Mind: Science and the Continuity of Consciousness beyond the Brain.* Inner Traditions.
and
Laszlo, E. & Peake, A. "The Evidence for Reincarnation: Scientifically Documented True Stories That Prove Past Lives Are Real." *Conscious Lifestyle.* https://www.consciouslifestylemag.com/reincarnation-stories-proof-past-life/

89. Ibid

90. – "Ensoulment." Wikipedia. https://en.wikipedia.org/wiki/Ensoulment

91. Campbell, J. 2014. "Intuition: Knowing without Knowing How We Know." *Farther to Go!* https://farthertogo.com/intuition-knowing-without-knowing-know/
and
Kahneman, D. 2001. *Thinking, Fast and Slow.* Farrar, Straus and Giroux.

92. Bargh, J. 2017. *Before You Know It: The Unconscious Reasons We Do What We Do.* Atria Books.

93. Ibid

94. Taylor, E. 2009. *Mind Programming: From Persuasion and Brainwashing to Self-Help and Practical Metaphysics.* Carlsbad, CA: Hay House.

95. Padgett, J. & Seaberg, M. 2014. *Struck By Genius: How a Brain Injury Made Me a Mathematical Marvel.* Mariner Books.

96. Oakes, L. "Psychic Knowing." *Healing Crystals for You.* https://www.healing-crystals-for-you.com/psychic-knowing.html

97. Jung, C.G. 1981. *The Archetypes and the Collective Unconscious.* Princeton University Press.

98. Staff. 2011. "Great Moments in Intuition: A Timeline." *O, The Oprah Magazine.* August 2011. https://www.oprah.com/spirit/a-history-of-intuition-intuition-timeline/all#ixzz5nC6VqVlo

99. Jen. 2021. "Listen to Your Heart and Trust Your Gut with These 20 Intuition Quotes." *Saying Images.* https://sayingimages.com/intuition-quotes/

100. McRaney, D. 2011. *You Are Not So Smart: Why You Have Too Many Friends on Facebook, Why Your Memory Is Mostly Fiction, and 46 Other Ways You're Deluding Yourself.* Gotham.

101. Shermer, M. 2014. "Anomalous Events That Can Shake One's Skepticism to the Core." *Scientific American.* October 1, 2014. https://www.scientificamerican.com/article/anomalous-events-that-can-shake-one-s-skepticism-to-the-core/
and
Shermer, M. 2014. "Infrequencies: I just witnessed an event so mysterious that it shook my skepticism." *Michael Shermer.* October 2014. https://michaelshermer.com/sciam-columns/infrequencies/

102. Mandino, O. 1990. *A Better Way to Live.* Bantam.

103. Deer, L. & Erdoes, R. 1972. *Lame Deer, Seeker of Visions.* Simon & Schuster.

104. Billings, L. 2019. "Atheism Is Inconsistent with the Scientific Method, Prizewinning Physicist Says." *Scientific American.* March 20, 2019. https://www.scientificamerican.com/ article/atheism-is-inconsistent-with-the-scientific-method-prizewinning-physicist-says/

105. Rainey, S. 2018. "All Together Now: Singing Is Good for Your Body and Soul: As Scientists Show That Choir Practice Is Healthier Than Yoga, Sarah Rainey – Who Does Both – Praises the Power of Song." *Waldorf Today.* https://www. waldorftoday.com/2018/10/all-together-now-singing-is-good-for-your-body-and-soul-as-scientists-show-that-choir-practice-is-healthier-than-yoga-sarah-rainey-who-does-both-praises-the-power-of-song/

106. Pattillo, C.G.S., & Itano, J. 2001. "Laughter is the Best Medicine." *Oncology Nursing Update, American Journal of Nursing.* April 2001.

107. Stratton, A. 2010. "Gordon Brown Says Catholics Can Be UK's Conscience." *The Guardian.* April 1, 2010. https:// www.theguardian.com/uk/2010/apr/01/gordon-brown-catholics-uk-conscience

# Acknowledgements

It is not possible to write a book without building on the backs of so many who have gone before. To all of those who contributed to my understanding and education, thank you. That said, a special thank you is due to those who lent their time to me in my endeavor to understand their work and the implications thereof.

I also owe a special debt of gratitude to my readers. Many of them contributed ideas and thoughts that helped flesh out my story, but two specifically aided in an important way. Thank you, Richard Kielbon and William Taylor.

I am also grateful for my lovely wife Ravinder who has lent immense aid in the editing process, as well as assisting me during the incubation and chrysalis stages that led to the development of this book.

As always, my gratitude to Lois and Roy Bey, for without their support none of my work over the past thirty years would have happened.

Lastly, I am grateful to all of you who have chosen to invest your time and energy in reading my books. You have deeply honored me by doing so. Thank you.

# About Eldon Taylor

Eldon Taylor has made a lifelong study of the human mind and has earned doctoral degrees in psychology and metaphysics. He is a Fellow with the American Psychotherapy Association (APA) and an interdenominational minister.

Eldon was a practicing criminalist for over ten years while completing his education. He supervised and conducted investigations and testing to detect deception. His earliest work with changing inner beliefs was conducted from this setting, including a double-blind study conducted at the Utah State Prison from 1986 to 1987.

Eldon is president and director of Progressive Awareness Research, Inc. For more than 35 years, his books, audio and video programs, lectures, and radio and television appearances have approached personal empowerment from the cornerstone perspective of forgiveness, gratitude, and respect for all life. Eldon now lives in the countryside of Washington State with his wife and their two sons. Apart from his family and work, his true passion is horses.

**Visit Eldon's Website**
If you enjoyed this book and would like to learn more, please visit www.eldontaylor.com

# Previous Books by Eldon Taylor

Choices and Illusions: How Did I Get Where I Am, and How
Do I Get Where I Want to Be?
978-1-4019-4339-4

Mind Programming: From Persuasion and Brainwashing to
Self-Help and Practical Metaphysics
978-1-4019-2332-7

I Believe: When What You Believe Matters!
978-14019-3128-5

Self-Hypnosis and Subliminal Technology: A How-to Guide for
Personal Empowerment Tools You Can Use Anywhere!
978-1401937584

What Does That Mean? Exploring Mind, Meaning, and
Mysteries
978-1401923341

What If? The Challenge of Self-Realization
978-1401927387

Gotcha! The Subordination of Free Will
978-1620002360

Subliminal Learning: An Eclectic Approach
978-0940699001

Subliminal Communication: Emperor's Clothes or Panacea?
978-094069901X

Thinking Without Thinking: Who's in Control of Your Mind?
978-1559780339

Subliminal Technology: Unlocking the Power of Your Own
Mind
978-1559780371

Exclusively Fabricated Illusions
978-1559787802

Just Be: A Little Cowboy Philosophy
978-1-5597-8782-1

Simple Things and Simple Thoughts
978-0-9160-9518-5

Little Black Book
978-0-9160-9517-7

Wellness: Just a State of Mind?
978-1-5597-8034-7

Change Without Thinking
978-4019-2695-3

Motivational Nudges to Empower Your Life
978-1-6200-0374-9

Plus, hundreds of audio and video programs in multiple
languages.

Please visit: **www.eldontaylor.com**

# O-BOOKS

# SPIRITUALITY

O is a symbol of the world, of oneness and unity; this eye represents knowledge and insight. We publish titles on general spirituality and living a spiritual life. We aim to inform and help you on your own journey in this life.
If you have enjoyed this book, why not tell other readers by posting a review on your preferred book site?

**Recent bestsellers from O-Books are:**

### Heart of Tantric Sex
Diana Richardson
Revealing Eastern secrets of deep love and intimacy to Western couples.
Paperback: 978-1-90381-637-0 ebook: 978-1-84694-637-0

### Crystal Prescriptions
The A-Z guide to over 1,200 symptoms and their healing crystals
Judy Hall
The first in the popular series of eight books, this handy little guide is packed as tight as a pill-bottle with crystal remedies for ailments.
Paperback: 978-1-90504-740-6 ebook: 978-1-84694-629-5

## Take Me To Truth
Undoing the Ego
Nouk Sanchez, Tomas Vieira
The best-selling step-by-step book on shedding the Ego, using the
teachings of *A Course In Miracles*.
Paperback: 978-1-84694-050-7 ebook: 978-1-84694-654-7


## The 7 Myths about Love...Actually!
The Journey from your HEAD to the HEART of your SOUL
Mike George
Smashes all the myths about LOVE.
Paperback: 978-1-84694-288-4 ebook: 978-1-84694-682-0


## The Holy Spirit's Interpretation of the New Testament
A Course in Understanding and Acceptance
Regina Dawn Akers
Following on from the strength of *A Course In Miracles*, NTI
teaches us how to experience the love and oneness of God.
Paperback: 978-1-84694-085-9 ebook: 978-1-78099-083-5


## The Message of A Course In Miracles
A translation of the Text in plain language
Elizabeth A. Cronkhite
A translation of *A Course In Miracles* into plain, everyday
language for anyone seeking inner peace. The companion
volume, *Practicing A Course In Miracles*, offers practical lessons
and mentoring.
Paperback: 978-1-84694-319-5 ebook: 978-1-84694-642-4

## Your Simple Path
Find Happiness in every step
Ian Tucker
A guide to helping us reconnect with what is really important in our lives.
Paperback: 978-1-78279-349-6 ebook: 978-1-78279-348-9

## 365 Days of Wisdom
Daily Messages To Inspire You Through The Year
Dadi Janki
Daily messages which cool the mind, warm the heart and guide you along your journey.
Paperback: 978-1-84694-863-3 ebook: 978-1-84694-864-0

## Body of Wisdom
Women's Spiritual Power and How it Serves
Hilary Hart
Bringing together the dreams and experiences of women across the world with today's most visionary spiritual teachers.
Paperback: 978-1-78099-696-7 ebook: 978-1-78099-695-0

## Dying to Be Free
From Enforced Secrecy to Near Death to True Transformation
Hannah Robinson
After an unexpected accident and near-death experience, Hannah Robinson found herself radically transforming her life, while a remarkable new insight altered her relationship with her father, a practising Catholic priest.
Paperback: 978-1-78535-254-6 ebook: 978-1-78535-255-3

## The Ecology of the Soul
A Manual of Peace, Power and Personal Growth for Real People
in the Real World
Aidan Walker
Balance your own inner Ecology of the Soul to regain your
natural state of peace, power and wellbeing.
Paperback: 978-1-78279-850-7 ebook: 978-1-78279-849-1

## Not I, Not other than I
The Life and Teachings of Russel Williams
Steve Taylor, Russel Williams
The miraculous life and inspiring teachings of one of the World's
greatest living Sages.
Paperback: 978-1-78279-729-6 ebook: 978-1-78279-728-9

## On the Other Side of Love
A woman's unconventional journey towards wisdom
Muriel Maufroy
When life has lost all meaning, what do you do?
Paperback: 978-1-78535-281-2 ebook: 978-1-78535-282-9

## Practicing A Course In Miracles
A translation of the Workbook in plain language, with
mentor's notes
Elizabeth A. Cronkhite
The practical second and third volumes of The Plain-Language
*A Course In Miracles.*
Paperback: 978-1-84694-403-1 ebook: 978-1-78099-072-9

## Quantum Bliss
The Quantum Mechanics of Happiness, Abundance, and Health
George S. Mentz
*Quantum Bliss* is the breakthrough summary of success and spirituality secrets that customers have been waiting for.
Paperback: 978-1-78535-203-4 ebook: 978-1-78535-204-1

## The Upside Down Mountain
Mags MacKean
A must-read for anyone weary of chasing success and happiness – one woman's inspirational journey swapping the uphill slog for the downhill slope.
Paperback: 978-1-78535-171-6 ebook: 978-1-78535-172-3

## Your Personal Tuning Fork
The Endocrine System
Deborah Bates
Discover your body's health secret, the endocrine system, and 'twang' your way to sustainable health!
Paperback: 978-1-84694-503-8 ebook: 978-1-78099-697-4

Readers of ebooks can buy or view any of these bestsellers by clicking on the live link in the title. Most titles are published in paperback and as an ebook. Paperbacks are available in traditional bookshops. Both print and ebook formats are available online.
Find more titles and sign up to our readers' newsletter at http://www.johnhuntpublishing.com/mind-body-spirit
Follow us on Facebook at https://www.facebook.com/OBooks/
and Twitter at https://twitter.com/obooks